LIFE
The Manual

LIFE
The Manual

Dr. Frank Sovinsky
Life: The Manual

Library of Congress Control Number: 2002091727

ISBN 0-9716958-0-6
Literary Press Publishing

Literary Press

3857 Birch Street, Suite 702
Newport Beach, California 92660

CONTENTS

DEDICATION

This book is dedicated to the memory of my parents. Detective Frank L. Sovinsky who taught me that even if the bad guys appear to be winning some of the time, doing the right thing wins all of the time. To my mother Anne whose unconditional love gave me the courage to rise above my perceived limitations and reach for my star.

ACKNOWLEDGEMENTS

I am blessed with incredible relationships. The most significant being the one I enjoy with my best friend, my wife, Cathy, who has taught me the meaning of love. Thank you to Dr. Tim and Robin Chaffin, your friendship and loyalty are living examples of spirituality. I am grateful to Dr. Cecile Thackeray for being my intuitive, provocative, and demanding muse. Thanks to Dr. Doug Sea for his friendship and willingness to tell me his truth.

A special thanks to Robert Woodcox for his guidance and creative contributions that inspired this fledgling writer. Thanks for contributing your mind, body and spirit as you made this work a part of you.

Thank you Dr. Arlan Fuhr for teaching me the art and science of Chiropractic. I want to acknowledge Robert Alderman for his persistent interest in my coaching career, and for introducing me to the world of behavioral assessments. Thanks to Bill Bonnstetter for his vision that humankind can learn to appreciate behavioral diversity.

I am indebted to my coaching clients for their life examples, that have become an intimate part of the Peak Performance Process. I am grateful to my patients in Lodi, California, for trusting me as your Chiropractor and understanding that it was time for me to move on.

Thanks to Cindy Frazier and Drs. Joe Fiore, Bob Leib, Mark Soccio and Tim Schroeder for their contributions to this book.

Hello, I'm Dr. Frank Sovinsky

But then you probably knew that from the cover. I sincerely hope that your life is complete, you feel total peace of mind and you are 100% fulfilled. If you feel something less than wonderful, you probably picked up this book because you are missing something in your life; it could be little things or it could be a dramatic void.

Unfortunately, we don't come with instruction manuals on how to achieve peace of mind and fulfillment. We pick up bits and pieces from everyone around us on our journey through life, from our parents and family, then our friends, teachers, people in the church, or the coach on the soccer team. All of this information can be truly bewildering and often in conflict. For that reason, I decided to write, *LIFE: The Manual*, because life really isn't all that complicated. You started out perfect and somewhere along the way, you and I and everyone else got sidetracked. Know this though: The only things keeping us from our perfection, and therefore complete fulfillment, are our own interferences, the ones we've either set up for ourselves, or the stumbling blocks that others have thrown in our path — all just things we have yet to remove.

Yes, I know, you're reasonably successful; if you weren't, you wouldn't have picked up this book. Perhaps you've even reached the pinnacle of your chosen profession. You might be a leader in your community or just an occasional attendee at your child's school PTA meetings.

Like many people, you work hard, give your best effort, and try to be a good person and hope that you find happiness along the way. If you have done a reasonable job in all of these endeavors, you will probably be satisfied to see your children grow up to be healthy, normal adults who, in turn, are happy and successful. You are most likely looking forward to a financially secure retirement with your health intact. You don't mind working hard, yet someday you would probably like to work less and enjoy life more and take some long time outs.

Am I close?

Perhaps you've done better than most, in terms of your financial success. You have been able to buy a large comfortable home, two or three cars, a boat perhaps? In short, you are surrounded by luxury and yet you feel there is still a void in your life, perhaps many. These missing elements could be love, friendship, self-esteem, the respect of your children or your co-workers, questions about your spirituality, or a host of any of the other important aspects of life. Countless people have achieved ultimate financial success and lived miserable emotional existences. Conversely, some happy people live on the edge of financial ruin. The majority of people live somewhere in between, a sort of twilight existence, with fleeting moments of happiness and/or illuminations that never quite fulfill them completely.

The message contained in this book is quite simple: **YOU CAN HAVE IT ALL, FULFILLMENT, HAPPINESS AND MONEY.** This book is your gateway, your key to the life you want to design.

Before I begin to take you on a journey of self-discovery and down the road to an extraordinary life filled with everything you need and want, one of complete fulfillment, success and abundance, take a moment to answer one question in your own handwriting. Before you put pen to paper though, stop and take a deep breath and think about your answer seriously for a moment. Be brutally honest; no one is going to read it but you. Then we will begin.

Question:

Describe your perfect day: If you had more money than you needed and you could do whatever you wanted to do, whether that was lying in a hammock all day or becoming an astronaut, what would you do? What would a perfect day in your life look like? In other words, what do you really want? (Feel free to write your answer in the space provided.)

Answer:

–

Done? Good. Now hold that thought for a while, we will be coming back to it because, with the help of this book, that perfect day is where you are going.

So far, you know my name, but not what I do. I am a Personal Performance Coach. "What do you really want?" is the first question I ask each of my clients before we begin working together. For some the answer is freedom, for others it might be security and love, and still for others it might be wealth. It is important for me to know this before I begin to coach them so that I can understand what it is they want to OBTAIN and what they want to ATTAIN. The two are quite different, but related. OBTAINING is the accumulation of possessions: money, homes, boats, cars, vacations, etc. ATTAINING is about fulfillment, peace of mind, loving, being loved, and harmony. The point of this book is to help you achieve a balance of both. If you don't already know this, it is entirely possible to PLAY AND GROW RICH, flourishing from the inside out, being fulfilled and living a life of purposeful passion.

I would like for you to consider me your surrogate coach for the duration of this book. If you do this, I will help push you to the top. My wish for you is that your dreams become reality, no matter who you are, or what challenge you are facing. Believe me, I already know your destiny and it is beyond your wildest imagination.

My own search for meaning and wealth involved the help of many others and led me to the study of ancient and contemporary ideas. As Sir Isaac Newton said, "If I have seen farther, it is by standing on the shoulders of giants." Here's my hand. Step up and see it for yourself.

Have you ever felt that empty spot in the pit of your stomach? You know, the one that needs to be filled with something or somebody? So have I, and that's when I started to look for answers to the big questions, "Who am I?" and "Why am I here?" My search for meaning and a thirst for knowledge led me to the disciplines of philosophy and psychology. I wanted to know what other people had discovered in their search for answers to these universal questions. In addition, my studies of the traditional philosophy of chiropractic, neuroscience, and quantum mechanics have given me a unique perspective concerning the *Bodymind* design.

I began my lifestyle coaching practice as a Doctor of Chiropractic in 1982. My mission was to teach others what I had been taught. Within seven years, my practice grew to become one of the largest in North America. This success was largely due to the "coaching" relationship that was established between my patients and me. Together, we found logical solutions to eliminate the issues that were holding many people back. This is also the basis for the plan we will develop for you. I left my practice in 1997 to devote my full attention to Performance Coaching. Graduating from Coach-U in 1998, I received further training from Target Training International where I earned my CPBA (Certified Professional Behavior Analyst), and a CPVA (Certified Professional Values Analyst).

What does a Personal Performance Coach do? Coaching provides a method of establishing goals. It includes finding and focusing on your strengths and discovering the soft spots or ineffectual traits, in your life that you may or may not be aware, are holding you back. The coaching process is one of accountability, integrity, commitment, and self-discipline. During our time together, I would like your permission to say things as "Frankly" as possible. I call this, "Frankly speaking."

If you read something in this book that hits you right between the egos, let it in. It is probably an important issue to confront. I apologize in advance if you are offended; it is not my intention. However, I will risk your approval to deliver the message. As your coach, I am here for support and to provoke deeper thinking and responses. This special relationship will move you further and faster than you ever thought possible. Don't stop until you have read the entire book and have completed the assessments because you are worth it. This coaching relationship is an opportunity to experiment so that you can find your way to a thriving life by following a daily strategy. I call this the PEAK PERFORMANCE PROCESS.

You may not think you need a strategy for daily life. After all, things are pretty much laid out for you already. You get up in the morning and if you have children, you get them ready for school, then you shower, dress, and drive yourself to work. At work, you perform the tasks in front of you and at night you come home and do everything you did in the morning in reverse. So, why would you need a strategy for daily life?

Well, consider this story. It's called, "How to boil a frog."

You may never have eaten frog, but plenty of people have had frog legs (actually, they are quite good). To serve them, one must par boil them first, then fry them. As you might imagine, if you were the chef and you just tossed a frog into a pot of boiling water, he would jump right back out. So, the secret is to trick them. To do this you prepare a pot of room temperature water. You place the frog in the water and he is complacent. Now, you turn the heat on under the pot, ever-so-slightly. After a few minutes, the frog is doing the back stroke in your pot, feeling quite comfortable, as if in a spa. When the frog is really comfortable, you turn up the heat ever-so-slightly, again. Now, you repeat the process until the water is boiling, having lulled the frog into oblivion. As long as you increase the heat in very small increments, the frog never notices.

Are you that frog?

Mind-less activity and routine can cause you to lose connection with your purpose and destiny. It's the same as driving down a familiar stretch of highway and suddenly realizing you have been on automatic pilot and can't remember the past ten minutes. When we are asleep at the wheel of life, we miss incredible parts of the trip. Our focus is fuzzy and we are rarely connected to our life. TAKE CHARGE; STOP THE MUNDANE RITUALS.

Once, when I was struggling, frustrated, bored and stuck, someone told me, "Just be happy, and if it isn't broke don't fix it." Well, that got my attention. At that very moment I adopted a different slogan, "If it ain't broke, break it." Stop the madness of sameness. Leap with all of your strength out of the pot before you are boiled in the soup of mediocrity. Decide to do it now, even if you are not sure where you're jumping. Remember, as your Coach, I am here with a towel and a plan just for you.

When you are finished reading this book for the day, I want you to go outside and look at the sky, the stars, the clouds, the trees and plants. Listen to the wildlife as they dance with their destinies, take a breath and realize your connection to creation. You are a part of this perfect design.

Before you can begin to tap into your strengths and design the life and lifestyle you want, it is important to know where you stand right now. It's a bit like walking into a giant shopping mall not knowing where the shoe store is that you want to visit. Rather than venturing down one part of the mall after another on a hit and miss mission, wouldn't it be easier to go to the directory, the one that shows a big red dot next to the words, "You are here"? The only difference in these analogies is that in life, you don't have a directory; you didn't come with a manual, and so, you may not even know where you are right now. You may not realize what your true strengths are, what your hidden passions might be, or even what your weaknesses are. Even if you know, you may have buried your weaknesses in your subconscious, preferring, as most others, not to deal with them. Moreover, like many others, you may not be taking ownership of your own talents and strengths, though others around you may readily see them.

I want you to consider this book your directory, as well as your map to reaching your maximum potential—your peak mental, physical and spiritual performance—your life manual.

If you are to achieve this, you must first take a trip of self-discovery, wherein you find out just who you really are. THIS WILL BE ACCOMPLISHED BY ANSWERING QUESTIONS IN SOME ASSESSMENTS early in this book. These assessments are quite unique and you will be astounded at how revealing they are. Though they are brief, it is imperative that you take the time and answer them carefully and HONESTLY. After you've done this, together we will analyze your scores and provide you with customized coaching insights that will begin to set you on a path of true enlightenment and ultimately a physical, mental and spiritual state that is beyond your comprehension at this moment.

This book is also comprised of principles and an action plan, similar to those that have been used by hundreds of coaches and thousands of their clients in this country over the last ten years, to successfully help people obtain the lifestyle they desired and the freedom to live life on their own terms.

Before we begin, I would ask two things of you. First, as I have requested, consider me your own Personal Performance Coach. Try to envision yourself sitting across from me as you read this book and we have a dialogue. Second, keep an open mind. If only for the time it takes to read this book. Suspend all of your beliefs about personal growth, success strategies, and health care. Pretend that anything is possible—anything!

I am about to take you on an incredible journey. Fasten your seat belts, here we go.

PART I
Getting To Know You

You are perfect! Don't look around the room. I'm talking to you. You heard me right, you are perfect. You already have all the talent, creativity, intuition, and genius you need to be prosperous. You have the ability to surround yourself with all of the abundance you could ever want. And you have the ability to experience **complete peace of mind.**

THE ONLY PROBLEM IS THAT YOU ARE INTERFERING WITH YOUR PERFECTION, IN ONE WAY OR ANOTHER.

We are about to change all that and bring you full circle back to where you started; sort of erasing the blackboard, wiping it down, first with a dry erasure and then with a clean, wet cloth. In order to achieve this, you must keep an open mind. One of my favorite bumper stickers reads, "The mind is like a parachute, they both work better when opened."

You see, we were all designed to be perfect, to be well, happy, and fulfilled—perfection is the normal order of things. This is the naturally occurring state of existence, not the stressful, competitive, worrying state you may be experiencing now.

I can hear you as if we were sitting together, "Yeah, sure. If I am so perfect, why am I about to get a divorce? Why don't my children respect me? Why can't I get that promotion? Why are my sales down? Why am I unhappy so often? Why do I get sick? Why is my best friend angry with me?" or words to that effect. Am I right?

I am going to answer you shortly, but before I do, let me give you a great mind-opening tip: Instead of always asking, "Why?" start, today, to ask, "What is the meaning of this for me?" and, "What can I do about it?" Think about it. When Newton was sitting under that tree and the apple fell on his head, if he had asked, "Why?" instead of, "What is the meaning of this for me?" and "What can I do about it?" we might all still be riding horse-drawn carts instead of soaring to the moon and beyond. From this day forward, every time you have the urge to ask, "Why?" instead ask: "What is the meaning of this for me, and what can I do about it?"

If you hear a little voice say, "I can't do this, or I can't do that." STOP and ask, "What CAN I do?" You will be amazed at how quickly you will begin to see life in sharper focus. Ideas will begin to come to you that would never have occurred by asking, "Why?"

This Peak Performance Program is simple, so simple you may be tempted to dismiss it. I hope you won't do that because everything that is truly astounding, wonderful and beautiful in this world is simple. It's when we over analyze and complicate things that we build our roadblocks across our path to success. Winston Churchill observed: "The simple things are the greatest things in life." Once you begin to unlock the real you, you will see that my program makes perfect sense.

Finally, as your surrogate coach, I suggest you USE this book. I know, you've been told since you were a little child to respect books, not to mark in them or bend the pages, but I am now giving you permission to mark it up with notes, bend the pages back so you'll be able to find important concepts quickly, write in it and use sticky notes if you wish. Use a highlighter. Consider this a WORKBOOK, as well as a textbook, a keepsake, a place to make notations. A manual for life. In fact, there will be some assessments that you will be filling out in this book, so you will have to write in it anyway. I encourage you to treat this as a learning TOOL.

You may have already noticed my grammatical "no-nos." This is not from my lack of English skills. When you see words that are WRITTEN IN ALL CAPS, I am raising my voice a little like in an email. This is not out of anger. It is to gain your attention more fully and to accent a particularly important word or concept.

A couple of years ago, while traveling in Egypt, I came upon an Egyptian hieroglyph that contained the image of Thoth,the scribe, writing the name of the pharaoh in the Tree of Life. This was a privilege that only the pharaoh's enjoyed. This particular cartouche had special meaning. Our guide interpreted it to mean, "Unless it is written, it doesn't exist." That powerful statement moved me to consider the impact of writing things down.

Your answers to these questions and the ones in our upcoming assessments could be the writings on your own Tree of Life. It is important to make a connection between your thoughts and dreams, and the reality that is your life. The thoughts that you have are indeed the most powerful in nature, yet unless they become specific and are transformed into action, they remain abstractions, vague intentions, goals never realized.

Before we begin, here are the fifteen questions I ask my clients when they first meet with me. When you reveal your thoughts you gain perceptive, you begin to trust yourself and others more. This self-disclosure exercise is a proclamation that you are willing and able to step up to the plate. Go ahead, make some more marks in this book now, and fill them out. We will come back to them later. When you have finished the book, you can answer them again and I guarantee you, your answers will be quite different. You may have a little trouble answering some of them, just do the best you can. Be open and honest.

Reader questionnaire

I want to help you achieve your next level; more fun, more profit, and more life. Please answer the following questions briefly. Be honest. No one else will see them but you.

1. Why are you reading this book?

2. What motivates you?

3. What is your life long dream?

4. Where do you really excel?

5. Are you aware of any "soft spots" that hold you back?

6. What are some of your healthy sources of energy...
   (exercise, proper diet, a challenge, family, spirituality, etc.)?

7. Where do you get energy that doesn't serve you, or
   is actually unhealthy...(caffeine, competition, stress,
   deadlines, crisis, drugs, etc.)?

8. What consumes your time that does not give you a wonderful PRESENT or FUTURE?

9. How willing are you to make substantial changes?

10. How will you know how effective our coaching has been?

Finish the following statements:
11. If you really knew me_____

12. I am trying to give the impression that_____

13. I'm afraid you'll think I'm_____

14. I am avoiding_____

15. I want to tell you_____

Good work. There are just a few insights that I would like to share with you as a result of looking over your responses. This entire process includes reading the book and doing the assessments. It will probably take more energy than you currently have in reserve, so here is a quick way to power-up.

Look at your response to question #6. Add more of these activities and interactions. Now pay attention to questions #7 and #8 because these behaviors suck your life marrow. Stop doing them and start doing the energizers that really work for you (#6). You might want to write down the positive sources of energy on a separate piece of paper or index card to remind you. Be creative, use different colors of paper and ink. You could also make them the screen saver on your computer. The point is to remind yourself until it is a habit.

THE PEAK PERFORMANCE PROCESS

In the adrenaline-charged world of competitive sports, discipline, training, and brilliant performances separate the exceptional athlete from the pack. Interviews with excellent athletes prove that a Peak Performance Process is the foundation of every accomplished competitor.

You must approach your life with this same commitment and passion if you are to achieve your dreams. Forethought, dedication, and focused actions separate those who *thrive* from those who just survive. Every successful man and woman that I have had the privilege to coach, has developed his or her own unique Peak Performance Process. Master this process and you will CREATE and SUSTAIN success.

PEAK
The point of greatest intensity and personal development.

PERFORMANCE
Actions taken to achieve your peak.

PROCESS
A continuous series of actions and changes
toward personal growth.

This book is not a ten day miracle plan for peak performance, happiness or fulfillment. It is a manual for your life. The Peak Performance Plan is the beginning of your new life. The plan incorporates specific and very unique assessments, as I have already mentioned, that you will be taking to help you define **who you are, what you are doing here** and **what your**

passions in life might be, if you don't already know. In addition to these eye-opening assessments, there are specific guidelines, general information, my opinions and some miscellaneous thoughts. In all, by the time you finish reading all of this, you will realize that you have just gone through the description of a Peak Performance IN LIFE. The process begins right now.

In sports and in the quest for fulfillment, you have the choice to *exist* as a spectator, or *persist* as a player. Spectators sit in relative comfort, dreaming of glory, vicariously experiencing the realities of others. They spend their lives wishing at the well of futility. Players leap at the chance to pursue their dreams, risking it all to gain soul-stirring satisfaction. Athletes I have interviewed say something like this, "When I am on, I am completely immersed in a flow. Everything comes together. It all just works for me." They go on to describe a clearing of the "field" and a connectedness of mind, body and spirit. It does not matter if they win or lose. The performance process invigorates them and that is why they choose to live as a player, willing to risk it all to capture their dreams. They can never be content to live the predictable existence of a spectator. Most of them SEE the outcome and BELIEVE it will happen. Confidence is everything.

I recently listened to a 2002 Winter Games Olympian tell a reporter that since the age of five, in her mind, she was a gold medalist. On the day of the competition, she was not fearful of failure because she was already a winner. Like most athletes, she felt honored to be a part of the games. She was ecstatic to have the opportunity to make her dream breathe and come alive.

My purpose for using sports analogies to describe the Peak Performance Process is to inspire and encourage you. I am hopeful that you have experienced an amazing afternoon of golf or a perfect day of skiing. If you have not yet tasted this nectar, then get ready for the best days of your life. When you tap the "fire within", all parts of your life ignite.

This brings us to my next point: **universal principles.** By definition, they exist in every human endeavor. Therefore, you can apply the same disciplines that top athletes practice and implement them in your own pursuit of the gold. And, I make no distinction between your work life and your playtime because wherever you go, there you are. We can draw lessons learned from one area to boost the performance of the other. I will tell you how a little later.

If, at any time while you are reading this book, you hear a voice in your head shouting, "Yeah, but, you don't know how hard it is." or, "Yeah but, dude, I'm doing the best I can." or some similar dribble, tell yourself to snap out of it! Imagine that you and I are sitting across from each other and just as you begin to recite your vintage "whines," you hear my trademark response, "I care, but not that much." I do care, I want your life to be everything you want it to be, it's just that neither of us has the time to waste talking trash.

Are you with me? By the way, while you have been thinking about making your life exceptional, there are men and women, just like you, succeeding in their lives at this very moment by applying these simple principles. In our coaching sessions they cannot wait to tell me how the Peak Performance Process has transformed their lives. They all experience a mind/body connection that germinates ideas, catalyzes decisions, and compels action. They embrace adversity and challenge with a creative, confident spirit. Peak performers view each day as a new opportunity to DO and BE their best. They are sucking the marrow out of life.

On the other end of the spectrum, opposite the polished players, there are those who take to the field in a nonchalant manner. These neophytes distract themselves looking for the "silver bullet" or fast track to success or happiness. They hope that they can skip the drudgery of practice and the seasoning of experience.

The wishful, seductive illusion of an "overnight success," kills the legitimate aspirations of far too many people. The truth is, that in most cases, Peak Performing individuals work decades to be overnight successes. Of course exceptions exist, but do not covet their good fortune or waste time thinking about luck and it's role in life. (Oh, by the way, if you hand me a winning lottery ticket I will gladly accept it. However, you will not find me holding my breath or waiting at the mailbox to see if I am the "Publisher's Clearing House" grand prize winner).

As your coach, I strongly urge you to stop wishing for success and start accepting it. Like you, I am taking actions today that will guarantee an even better tomorrow.

If you want to take charge of your life, FROM THIS POINT FORWARD, THERE CAN BE NO ORDINARY MOMENTS. EVERY MOVEMENT AND THOUGHT IS CONNECTED TO EACH OTHER. YOUR LIFE WILL NOW UNFOLD AS A PROCESS, A PEAK PERFORMANCE PROCESS!

This process is a natural progression from where you are now to where you want to be. It can be a gradual change or a fast-paced leap to your goals. Time is relative and a lot depends upon how you put to work the coaching insights that follow each assessment, and the momentum that you have going along with the intensity of that work.

The Peak Performance Process is how you become who you are, a winner. The young Olympian I referred to earlier trained for years; her competitions included wins and losses. It didn't matter that much to her because each day was a step closer to her dream. Her body developed, her *Bodymind* intelligence progressed, and her extrasensory attunement provided guidance. I want to remind you, also, to enjoy the *preparation*, the *performance* and the *polish* moments equally. The small achievements in your life often lead to the next evolutionary step in becoming all that you were born to be.

You have a limited amount of time to do what needs to be done. Each day is an opportunity to experiment and to play with destiny. Your purpose right now is to prepare and express your essence; the world is waiting to feel your impact. We are waiting to benefit from your efforts. How will the world be a better place because of you? What legacy are you going to leave? How willing are you to grab hold of the life you want? How far will you reach? How many times will you get up when you are knocked down? All champions have the same winning strategy; they simply get up one more time than they are knocked down. Do the math, drag your butt up off the ground, dust yourself off and get back in the game.

I must warn you though, this journey is not always comfortable. The comfort zone will no longer provide a refuge from the reality of life. You can no longer cruise the sofa or drive the recliner to TV land and be complacent. The Peak Performance Process will expose all of your limiting beliefs and soft spots. One by one you will eliminate them and add to your natural talents a host of refining skills. I have heard people say that we give birth to ideas and dreams. While I have never experienced the labor of childbirth, I have birthed success.

I can tell you that, like birth, there is the conception of a dream, followed by a gestation period of growth and then development, and, finally, the delivery event. My wish for you is that you get pregnant with your dream, carry it to term, and share it with the world.

The Peak Performance Process that we are designing for you contains three distinct phases. Each phase is a point in the cycle of advancement.

The cycle is as follows:

Phase One - **Preparation**
Phase Two - **Performance**
Phase Three - **Polish**

We will explore each phase separately a little later in the book. Right now, I want you to meet an extraordinary person, YOU.

You have already engaged the Preparation Phase just by picking up this book and reading this far. Every concept we discuss, each question you contemplate clears the way and fills in the missing pieces. You could interfere, but I doubt you will. Welcome to the rest of your life and to the process of growth and restoration of your perfect nature.

Do You Deserve To Be Happy?

What does "living the good life" mean? Is it being happy all the time? Alternatively, is it a complete and total sense of fulfillment? What is the difference? We live in a land of infinite possibilities and opportunities. American history is filled with awe-inspiring stories of ordinary people overcoming adversities and using the "perfection within" to accomplish remarkable goals. Some of us have come to believe that we DESERVE happiness.

"Do not go around saying that the world owes you a living: the world was here first."

-Mark Twain

Happiness is one of the six universal emotions. Because it is an emotion, it can enrich or deplete us by its impact. Just like fear and anger, each has its place and purpose and all three can pull us off course.

If there is one universal "want" it would be to be happy. But what exactly does that mean? Happy every moment? Ecstatic every day? A lifetime of happiness? And just what *is* happiness? Is it good health, security, being loved, loving someone, three square meals a day? A new red corvette?

I guess you can see how difficult it is to get your arms around happiness. To a homeless person, it could be as simple as a good meal and one night's sleep in a decent bed. The reason I bring this up is to demonstrate a very important point. This program is not about teaching you how to be "happy" everyday. It is about a much higher purpose—that of complete fulfillment in your life, fulfillment in your mental, physical and spiritual being. A life of abundance, both OBTAINED and ATTAINED. A life in complete balance.

Everyone wants to live the "good life" where our needs are fulfilled and our desires granted. We all want our efforts to be recognized and rewarded. We attend to our required studies and graduate from high school, then aspire to higher learning in order to obtain the requisite skills to succeed. After all, the good jobs are reserved for the highly educated and skillful, or so we have been told. How else can we acquire the house of our dreams, that nifty new car, send our children to the best schools? When we toil and struggle, we expect our just rewards, our paybacks.

Oddly enough, striving for happiness is just one small piece of life's puzzle. A life of profound emotional and physical well being, abundance, and peace of mind certainly contain moments and times of extraordinary happiness, but that is just one aspect of complete fulfillment.

The "pursuit of happiness" alone can be extremely shallow, never touching the profound life. Happiness can be like a promising rain in a drought that many times never reaches the soil, evaporating in a mist, not quite nurturing the seeds of destiny.

So it is with having happiness as our only goal in life. In America, we have come to believe that we have a *right* to happiness. Even the Constitution promises that we only have the right to *pursue* it, it doesn't say anywhere that you have the right to *have* it.

HAPPINESS IS NOT THE DESTINATION. It can give us encouragement and enrich our experiences, but it can not be the focus. Indeed, living a life of profound well being provides moments of exceptional happiness and a deep-rooted satisfaction, but only as the result of having a bigger purpose already.

When was the last time you had a sincere conversation with yourself? I don't mean the monologue wherein you hear, "I shoulda," "I coulda," "I woulda." If, if, if. And, if I were seven foot three, I'd be a star in the NBA, but I'm only five foot nine. No, I mean the living dialogue that asks and listens, not talks and yells; one that doesn't include any "ifs."

Now, take a moment to pause, a reflective moment, and answer the following questions about happiness. Write them in this book. Answer these questions from your heart and be completely honest with yourself. The simple act of writing things down can give you a sense of momentum that can help you to overcome inertia. That is one of the reasons I have encouraged you to write in this book, to make your notes and answers to the questions tangible and permanent.

To begin to understand the difference between mere happiness and profound well being, it is important to bring life to your answers. Here is an example of what I'm talking about.

Questions:

1. What does happiness mean to you?

2. Is it a feeling of pleasure that stimulates a lust for living?

3. Is it a deep sense of security that brings with it hope for tomorrow?

4. Are you worthy of happiness and good fortune?

5. How can you tell when you are happy? What is the evidence?

6. Does it involve others or can you feel it when you're alone?

7. When things are going right, do you get a sinking feeling that this just cannot last, it's too good to be true?

8. Have you been led to believe that GOOD FORTUNE has to be balanced by misfortune?

SEEKING HAPPINESS AND PLEASURE CAN ACTUALLY BE A REAL DISTRACTION IN YOUR JOURNEY TO ACHIEVE A MORE IMPORTANT OBJECTIVE—YOUR REAL POTENTIAL.

A feeling of happiness is the interpretation that our *Bodymind* gives to a person, situation or thing. Happiness is emotional and just like negative emotions, it is a perceived event. Happiness can be a very sensual experience. Your mind and body can light up. You can potentially feel each molecule vibrate to an ancient rhythm. It will come as no surprise that intense feelings of happiness have the exact same effect on your body as intense fear and rage. You become trapped in the moment and effectively block out mortgage worries, job loss, or problems with your spouse or children.

While diversions have a place in your life, they can never become a *way* of life. Problems, unless solved logically, become *Bodymind* malignancies eating away your life energy.

Can you think of someone right now who makes you happy? What is it about them that enables that to happen? How do you behave differently around them? What do they do or say that sets your mood swinging?

Now, imagine a place that you can go that makes you happy? What is it about this place? What is it about YOU in this place that is different?

Do you have a favorite thing, something that is yours that brings you happiness? Who are you when you look at it, touch it, smell it? Does it transport you to another time? How do you behave when you're in its presence?

I'm sure you've been pausing to reflect after each of these questions, it's fun to do so. Perhaps you were able to answer some of them quite clearly and quickly.

Now, I have a secret to share with you: people, places or things cannot make you happy! IT IS YOU WHO DECIDES, MOMENT-TO-MOMENT, EXPERIENCE-TO-EXPERIENCE, WHETHER TO BE FILLED WITH JOY OR NOT.

The next time you say, "He or she makes me so happy," or "Going to the mountains makes me happy to be alive," remember it is YOU who is actively co-creating the happiness you feel.

So much of our happiness is the result of our own choices. However, when our entire purpose for living is to be happy, we miss a life of true PROFOUND EMOTIONAL AND PHYSICAL WELL BEING. We fail to balance our desires for OBTAINING and ATTAINING things.

Unfortunately, our obsessions with happiness leave many of us feeling empty and cheated. We find ourselves settling for the crumbs of happiness when we could have the entire loaf of complete fulfillment.

We may have experienced happy moments but then, suddenly, out of nowhere, we can be hit in the face with the fist of disappointment—reality. Suddenly we are, again, rudely awakened and brought back to the "real world" where something or someone else is in control. We ask ourselves, "Why can't the good times ever last?"

WHAT DO YOU VALUE?

A well known principle of success is that when your head, heart and passion converge, your life attracts money and meaning. When my clients first hear this statement they say, "Yeah, but Dr. Frank, I can't really make a living reading, painting, or traveling." My response is, "YES, YOU CAN." The proof is found by closely observing the lives of the people who truly inspire you. They make success look so easy and effortless because of their focused playfulness. When asked to reveal their success secret, they usually state that what they DO for a living does not feel like work to them. You see, each of them has discovered that special spark that energizes his/her thoughts and makes his/her particular career activity a completely fulfilling performance.

It is important to begin our program for **Peak Performance** with an examination of your strengths and a plan to implement these passions immediately. I believe that the search for meaning begins with finding and fanning the fire within. Through the assessment that you will be taking shortly, we will identify a few of the things in life that really bring joy, excitement and spark to your life experience. This will be a part of your **Manual** for living and it will help you answer the second part of our question, "Why am I here?"

Deep down inside, everyone has a passion. Without it, it is nearly impossible to set goals and to dream infinite dreams. And without dreams and goals, we can not move from where we are to where we want to go. What typically happens is, at some point in your life, someone tells you that in order to get ahead in life, you have to "grow up." You probably interpreted this to mean work can't be fun. This comes as a severe shock to your playful, creative and intuitive nature. Your naturally balanced ego-system is thrown off course and you become splintered into two separate life strategies. One part of you pursues the task of making a living, while the other attempts to recover from the toil, all the while longing to be free. We learn to delay living until our financial goals are obtained and our family duties are met. We tell ourselves, "When the kids are raised and we are retired, life will be great." Some of us openly rebel and respond to this pressure by engaging in a lifestyle that is moment to moment, having experiences with no substance. There is a much simpler approach. That is to see your career as a part of your journey and not as a forced march of drudgery. When you are able to blend your passions with your daily performances, you simultaneously experience enjoyment and fulfillment.

You may be surprised at how simple it is to discover your inner passions. Let me ask you a few more questions. Why do you get out of bed in the morning? What is it that draws your energy and demands satisfaction? While it is true that you are unique in your specific passions, we all share a few basic ones. Psychologist Gordon Allport working with P.E. Vernon and G. Lindzey designed an assessment tool, "Study of Values," to help people understand what motivates them. Their pioneering work has inspired a host of assessments that can help determine a person's apparent motivators, as well as hidden or dormant passions. Today this instrument has evolved into an important business educational tool as a result of the influence of Bill J. Bonnstetter. The assessment that follows is a blend of the six basic values that Gordon Allport tested and Bill Bonnstetter refined, along with my coaching insights.

Shakespeare wrote, "To thine own self be true." He meant, know yourself. By knowing yourself, you have the ability to direct your life. Socrates suggested that if we do not take the time for self examination, then our life is not worth living. By answering the following questions and acting on the Coaching Insights, you will have taken the next step. The next step is to follow the advice of Aristotle, who said, "A life not planned is not worth examining."

Take the time to consider your answers but don't over analyze. I have found that the right answer for you is the first one that comes to mind. Circle TRUE if the statement is an accurate description of you today.

A

TRUE   I like to read books and magazines, even on topics not related to my profession.

TRUE   I enjoy learning new things and discovering hidden truths.

TRUE   I am interested in learning about how famous individuals dealt with life's adversities.

TRUE   I can recall quirky details and trivial facts on a variety of topics.

TRUE   Sometimes I watch a program, attend a lecture or read an article just for the pleasure of learning.

TRUE   I am usually the one who asks the question, "Why?"

TRUE   I feel that if a person is not learning, they are not living.

TRUE   I enjoy abstract, "What if" discussions.

TRUE   I get a sense that people see me as being smarter than most.

TRUE   I attend as many seminars as time permits.

Now total your TRUE responses for A_____.

B

TRUE   I seek a sense of flow and balance in my life.

TRUE   I enjoy the finer things in life.

TRUE   Nature quiets the chaos and refreshes my sense of self.

TRUE   Environmental preservation is a critical concern we all share.

TRUE   Most developers ruin the peace and tranquility of nature and should be more restricted.

TRUE   I am very aware of my surroundings.

TRUE   I am creative and enjoy expressing myself (e.g., art, music, interior design, cooking, writing).

TRUE   Most of the time, I am keenly aware of my inner feelings.

TRUE   I am on a continual quest for self improvement.

TRUE   I want my body and clothes to express my
            inner refinement.

Now total your TRUE responses for B_____.

C

TRUE   Money and possessions are a good indicator of
            success or failure.

TRUE   I look for practical down to earth approaches.

TRUE   I expect to have a return on my investments.

TRUE   If I put an effort forward, I expect something
            in return.

TRUE   I want to get my money's worth with every
            purchase.

TRUE   I purchase items based on their practicality
            and ability to hold their value.

TRUE   If I see an item that I recently purchased has
            gone on sale, I will return it and ask for the
            sale price.

TRUE   There is little doubt that money talks.

TRUE   Time is important to me, I do not appreciate
            someone wasting it.

TRUE   If I pay for a large soft drink, I expect it to be filled to the top with beverage, not foam.

Now total your TRUE responses for C_____.

D

TRUE   I need to take control of my own destiny.

TRUE   I am very competitive.

TRUE   I find it easy to make alliances that further my career or agenda.

TRUE   Status is important to me.

TRUE   I enjoy recognition.

TRUE   I like hanging out with highly motivated people.

TRUE   Setbacks are only temporary and make me even more determined.

TRUE   I am usually the driving force in any group.

TRUE   I must look out for number one.

TRUE   If somebody has to be in charge it might just as well be me.

Now total your TRUE responses for D_____.

E

TRUE   I hate to see others suffer and struggle.

TRUE   I rarely pass a homeless person without giving him money.

TRUE   I know some people consider me a sucker for a sob story.

TRUE   I really believe in the saying, " There, but for the grace of God, go I."

TRUE   People should always come first.

TRUE   Charities must be supported, it is our responsibility to take care of the less fortunate in society.

TRUE   I get upset with people who are always promoting themselves.

TRUE   I wish I could do more to help people.

TRUE   I love being a member of a team that is making a difference in the world.

TRUE   I have a hard time saying, "No," when asked to help.

Now total your TRUE responses for E_____.

F

TRUE   I see things as clearly as black and white.

TRUE   I will take the time to persuade someone to my view.

TRUE   I see myself as a spiritual being having a human experience.

TRUE   I feel very strongly about a right and a wrong way of doing things.

TRUE   I will gladly put energy into a worthy cause.

TRUE   If people would seek deeper growth and understanding, they would live a better life.

TRUE   I tend to hang out with people who share my views.

TRUE   I get frustrated when people refuse to see things the way I do.

TRUE   All of the meaningful rewards in life come from within.

TRUE   I have high standards that I strive to live by and I measure others accordingly.

Now total your TRUE responses for F_____.

Coaching Insights

By now, you have discovered that in each section there may have been at least one or two TRUE answers, because you are a blend of all of these values. What I would like you to do is focus your efforts on the sections in which you answered TRUE to five or more of the statements. Then circle or highlight the suggestions (immediate actions) that grab your attention and list them in the space provided (my choices). Refer to your list at least once a week. It is important to hold yourself accountable at a deeper, more personal level.

When you have finished, I want you to go back over the coaching suggestions (immediate actions) and highlight the one or two that cause your inner dialogue to say, "No way am I going to do that." I have discovered that when I experience a strong initial resistance to a suggestion, it is often an extraordinary opportunity to break free to the other side.

(A) THEORETICAL

If you answered TRUE to five or more or these questions, then you enjoy the intellectual process and pursuit of knowledge. Identifying, differentiating and systematizing information comes naturally to you. You may enjoy solving problems or mysteries. The quest for truth is continual along with the discovery of new and fresh concepts and you probably enjoy travel because it is a chance to learn and to discover.

Stressors: No ability to learn, shallow work, feeling that everything is already understood.

Present circumstance: If you are satisfied in your present career then here are a few suggestions to ignite your passion.

Immediate Actions:

- Attend seminars.
- Enroll in continuing education classes.
- Obtain advanced training in your present career and become the expert.
- Read books on a variety of subjects (perhaps as many as five at a time).
- Write down your ideas (start by journaling your reactions to what you are reading today).
- Visit museums.
- Surf the Internet for information on subjects that you find interesting.
- Listen to thought provoking talk shows, not emotional dribble.

My choices are:

Future possibilities: If you are thinking about changing your career, look into the following areas for satisfaction of this value: Researcher, teacher, scientist, research and development, exploration, new product launches, software creation, librarian, historian, and engineering.

B) AESTHETIC

If you answered TRUE to five or more of these questions, then the following information and action steps apply to you. You have a deep appreciation and enjoyment of form, harmony and beauty. You enjoy a personal or subjective experience. You interact with the beauty around you. This enjoyment can be from nature or from your material possessions. One of your goals in life is self-actualization. You interact with your environment and others on a level that most people don't understand. You have an appreciation of all impressions. You tend to reject that which causes pain and disharmony. Your focus is more on your subjective experience. You can connect with your inner vision and your intuition.

Stressors: Lack of form and harmony in your life, chaos, no personal growth, stifling of creativity.

Present circumstance: If you are satisfied in your present career, then here are a few suggestions to ignite your passion.

Immediate Actions:

• Trust and act upon your intuition.

- Immerse yourself in some medium of artistic expression (e.g., dance, playing a musical instrument).

- Self-development activities (e.g., books, tapes, programs, seminars).

- Attend art shows.

- Exercise.

- Photography.

- Go on nature walks.

My choices are:

Future possibilities: If you're thinking about changing your career look into the following areas for satisfaction of this value: Psychology, dance, acting, dentistry, landscape architect, cosmetic surgeon, interior decorator.

(C) UTILITARIAN

If you answered TRUE to five or more of these questions then the following information and action steps apply to you. You look for practicality in all areas of your life. You expect a return when you put time, energy, effort or money forward.

You are satisfied by creative application of your resources. You probably have a desire to surpass others by obtaining wealth. You may be conservative with your assets or a committed consumer. You can bring together various resources available in order to accomplish your goals. You may find enjoyment in producing goods, materials, services and marketing them for economic gain.

Stressors: Wasted resources, no return on investment, careers that reward seniority and/or have no incentives for production.

Present circumstance: If you are satisfied in your present career, then here are a few suggestions to ignite your passion.

Immediate Actions:
- Investing in the stock market (Online trading).

- Join an investment club.

- Begin collecting valuable antiques or works of art.

- Read the "Wall Street Journal" or "Entrepreneur."

- Look for ways to eliminate waste and excess in your home or business.

My choices are:

Future possibilities: If you are thinking about changing your career look into the following areas for satisfaction of this value: Entrepreneur, commissioned sales, managing a business.

(D) INDIVIDUAL / POLITICAL

If you answered TRUE to five or more of these questions then the following information and action steps apply to you. Your goal is to advance to the highest position in life and to take charge of your destiny and, perhaps, the destiny of others. You enjoy leading others and forming strategic alliances to advance your position. You engage in tactics, planning and carrying out winning strategies. Sometimes you form personal relationships to advance your position. Your goal is to assert yourself in having personal causes victorious.

Stressors: Actual or perceived threatening, diminishing or loss of position and power, losing a title, no possibility for further advancement, seniority system, controlled environment.

Present circumstance: If you are satisfied in your present career then here are a few suggestions to ignite your passion.

Immediate Actions:
- Look for opportunities to advance.

- Look for opportunities to lead a team.

- Search for key alliances in the community and corporate world that can assist you.

- Accept the public recognition and rewards that will come your way.

- Material possessions need to convey your authority (e.g., big desk, high-tech tools of the trade).

- Focus on becoming a better decision maker and communicator.

- Attend leadership training courses.

My choices are:

Future possibilities: If you're thinking about changing your career, look into the following areas for satisfaction: Banking, politics, law, business (corporate world of advancement), Chamber Of Commerce director, entrepreneur, management, sales manager, opportunities for quick advancement (ground floor of new venture).

(E) SOCIAL

If you answered TRUE to five or more of these questions then the following information and action steps apply to you. Your goal is to eliminate hate and conflict in the world. You invest yourself in others and enjoy assisting others in the fulfillment of their potentials. You are often regarded as a

43

selfless person. You are generous with your time, talents and resources. You can see the potential in others and want to help them develop. You are a champion of worthy causes. Your generosity is given with little or no expectation of return.

Stressors: Decisions which appear insensitive to people, too much emphasis on bottom-line results, downsizing, and self-promotion.

Present circumstance: If you are satisfied in your present career then here are a few suggestions to ignite your passion.

Immediate Actions:

- Community projects.

- Volunteer for causes that you believe will help mankind.

- Search for a people oriented vs. profit oriented environment.

- Look for new ways to help others and develop the talents you need to achieve that.

My choices are:

Future possibilities: If you are thinking about changing your career, look into the following areas for satisfaction: Arbitrator, minister, marriage/family therapist, social worker, compassion ministries, community projects organizer.

(F) TRADITIONAL / RELIGIOUS

If you answered TRUE to five or more of the questions then the following information and action steps apply to you. You look for the highest meaning in life. Your goal is to search for and find the highest value in life. You may have a strong spiritual connection. While you may pursue spirituality, it does not mean religion necessarily. Once you have found your system for living you will enjoy converting others to your cause or ideas.

Stressors: Opposition to your beliefs or causes, beliefs that conflict with yours, chaos, and self-serving philosophy.

Present circumstance: If you are satisfied in your present career then here are a few suggestions to ignite your passion.

Immediate Actions:

- Find a cause that is consistent with your personal set of beliefs.

- Look for an ethical and highly moral environment.

- Seek a mission.

• Pray or meditate more often.

• Join with people of like values, philosophical debates.

My choices are:

Future possibilities: If you are thinking about changing your career look into the following areas for satisfaction: Look for a company that is involved in the community, theological leadership, law enforcement, military, Rotarian activities, judicial system, ethics board membership, inspector, yoga instructor.

How Do You Behave?

Have you ever sat on a bench at a shopping mall and been entertained by the parade of shoppers? Did you find it humorous? So did the ancient Greeks and scholars of the Renaissance. The origin of the word "humorous" is rooted in an attempt to explain the diverse behaviors of people. They believed that the four humors: earth, air, fire and water influenced human emotion and behavior through the interaction of these distinct elements. While Carl Jung gave us four personality types, it was William Marston who published what we now call the DISC model of behavioral temperaments. The first behavioral assessment based on Marston's work was developed in the 1950's by Walter Clark. Most recently, Bill Bonnstetter, founder of Target Training International, has further developed, refined, researched and validated the behavioral assessment and today we have a variety of tools and assessments to better understand ourselves and enhance our appreciation of others.

Behavioral assessments are designed to let you see how others view you, and with this awareness, you can eliminate the stressful patterns that alienate people. Next you will be taking an introductory behavior and emotional assessment, or evaluation, if you prefer. This will help you build rapport with others naturally. I know that if you choose to develop your natural communication skills, you will feel the stress and conflict dissolve in your relationships. I want you to enjoy this assessment and what it says about you. LOOK FOR WAYS TO APPLY THIS INFORMATION IN YOUR DAILY INTERACTIONS WITH YOUR FAMILY AND CO-WORKERS.

1. Circle each word that describes you best. Choose carefully. Focus on how you are at work and, if you want, ask a few friends or co-workers to select which words they think describe you. This should only take two minutes.

2. Total the number you circled in each column and write that number at the bottom of each column.

3. The column(s) that you circled the most words in is your dominant style. Find that style and read about yourself.

4. Then read the communication tips for the styles different than you.

5. Apply these insights immediately.

Direct	Expressive	Relaxed	Conservative
Forceful	Trusting of others	Steady	Quality conscious
Decisive	Fun-loving	Patient	Attentive to detail
Take charge	Enthusiastic	Team-person	Analytical
Bottom-line	Optimistic	Reliable	Gather all facts
Likes challenge	Charismatic	Modest	Careful
Straight forward	Demonstrative	Consistent	Accurate
Ambitious	Good mixer	Loyal	Go by the book
Risk-taker	Animated	Amiable	Perfectionist
Aggressive	Convincing	Methodical	Reserved

D _____   I _____   S _____   C   _____

D stands for **Dominance:** Direct style, vision for future, high risk taker, straight forward, fast pace, short fuse, need to direct, self-starter, desire to win, forward looking, demanding, challenge-oriented.

If your score demonstrated a high number in the "D" column. You are a good problem solver who enjoys challenging assignments and likes confrontation. You thrive in situations where you can demonstrate power and authority. You are definitely interested in the bottom line and you drive for results. You have an ability to make decisions quickly. The higher your "D" factor the shorter your fuse. While you are a mosaic of feelings and emotions: anger, frustration and irritation can easily surface. You probably adapt to change readily and may set many high-risk goals. These goals will probably not be written down so I know you may be challenged by the exercises in this book. Remember, it is always your choice as to how you want to use this workbook, make it happen anyway you choose.

Your communication style is very direct. People always know where they stand with you. You are quick to challenge ideas that you don't agree with and you're willing to state unpopular opinions. If the conversation is going too slowly, your impatience may cause you to act or speak before thinking. You may have noticed a tendency to interrupt, to jump ahead or find yourself doing something else while you're talking with someone. In short, you probably are not a great listener. Others may perceive you as lacking tact and diplomacy, they may feel that you use fear as a motivator. You may be seen as someone who oversteps authority and directs too much. You may be challenged by a team culture at your workplace and if you are the boss, you may have a tendency to over delegate and under instruct. Your motto might be "Teamwork is a lot of people doing whatever I say."

Coaching insight:
Regardless of the task at hand, you will need people to achieve your goal. It is important to enroll people through cooperation, not coercion. This program is simple, if you want faster and greater results, here are some things to consider. Focus on developing better listening skills and you'll find that your directives will be followed. Your pace of speech may be

too fast for the majority of the population, slow down, annunciate and have dialogues with people. These do not have to be long drawn out conversations, simply get eye contact, demonstrate concerned attentiveness and watch your "bottom line" explode. Your tendency to juggle too many tasks at once can dissipate your focus. Another emotion that may surface and block your performance is the fear that someone will take advantage of you. Learn to discipline this emotion and you will achieve your objective. Competitive and aggressive exercise is a great stress reliever.

Communication tips:

When communicating with a person who is "D", remember they are looking for results, so be direct and to the point. Move quickly because they may make fast decisions. Do not dictate to them. Be careful not to over promise and under deliver. Do not try to overpower them and give them choices so that they feel as if they are in control. When you disagree, make sure that it is about the facts or the idea, not the person. Remember, they are interested in the bottom line and appreciate bulleted correspondence.

I stands for **Influence:** Outgoing, people oriented, creative problem solver, verbalizes articulately, positive sense of humor, motivates others, negotiates conflict as a team player, wears his heart on his sleeve.

If your score demonstrated a high number in the "I" column, you enjoy experiences and a rapid change of pace. You are humorous and fun loving. You have a unique ability to make others feel welcome and included. Trusting strangers is a natural extension of who you are. You are good at persuading people and talking them into your point of view. You are very people oriented and enjoy working with a team and interacting. You are highly contactable and people enjoy sharing things with you. You have an ability to see the "big dream" and communicate it. You are highly optimistic and people find that refreshing. Change may occur in your life without you even noticing it. You like new experiences and do not enjoy routines. When it comes to goal setting, you may have a challenge planning and attending to the details. I invite you to use colored pens, highlighters that are aromatic, and make bold expressions of yourself in this workbook.

Your communication style is demonstrative. You enjoy talking at length and are very personable. Your pace of speech is rapid and may be a challenge for people. Because you're very talkative, you guessed it, you're not the greatest listener. You may be quiet while the other person is talking, but you'll probably be thinking about what you are going to say next. When you talk you have a tendency to use a lot of big gestures and many facial expressions. People may perceive you as disorganized, inattentive to detail and impulsive. You have a tendency to talk before thinking.

Coaching insight:
Your personable manner is an asset. You will need to appreciate follow-up and attention to details. Slow down and think before you respond to a question, and if you have nothing to say, try silence for a change. There are times when your optimism can be seen as superficial. Remember, some people take longer to process information. Sometimes you lose track of time and find yourself late or hurried, this may be

interpreted as lackadaisical. Make sure that you plan all of your business presentations, so that you do not appear to be flying by the seat of your pants or that your ideas are not well thought out. We are looking at how others perceive you and with this awareness you can eliminate any block to cooperation. Work on your listening skills and you'll find a receptive audience. Your need to be liked and loved may act as a performance block.

Communication tips:

When communicating with a person who is "I", be personal and have fun. Allow them to talk and to tell their story. This individual is looking for an experience. Make sure that you talk about people. Give them recognition. Let them talk more than you. If it is important that they receive detailed information, paint the big picture and let them take the detailed data with them.

S stands for **Steadiness:** Supporter, dependable, likes closure, finish what they start, loyal, service oriented, good listener, empathetic, calming, logical and step-wise thinker.

If your score demonstrated a high number in the "S" column, you are very loyal to those that you identify with and long service is deemed important to you. Family and relationships are very important to you. You are stealth when it comes to demonstrating your feelings until you trust the person. You have tenacity for order and prefer secure situations. You have a natural ability to organize tasks and you are a good planner. In the work environment, you enjoy a slower pace and when given tasks, you would prefer to complete one before starting another. You may do the work yourself rather than to delegate it and, at times, may lack a sense of urgency. You may have a challenge prioritizing and shifting your attention from one task to another. You enjoy security and require more sleep than others.

Your communication style is warm and friendly. You demonstrate exceptional listening skills. People notice a very steady pace and a smile that reaches your eyes. You are patient and empathetic with others and you have an uncanny ability to see another person's point of view. You would make a good ambassador because you can calm and stabilize others, and you can mask your emotions. People often comment on how nice you are and it is true. You are a great conversationalist if someone else has initiated the dialogue. However, when asked a question , you may deliberate too long, as you search for the correct response.

Coaching insight:

Your listening skills are remarkable; your challenge is to respond. People who are accustomed to a more demonstrative interaction may perceive you as being moody. You may need to show more enthusiasm when communicating and make sure that you are more direct. You probably find that change is definitely not your strength and that you need much preparation to switch gears. While you are very loyal, if pushed too long, too hard, then, look out. If you are wronged you have a tendency to hold a grudge. You may appear too structured to some people and they may wish that you could lighten up. One thing to watch for is being too agreeable, try saying, "No" a little more often. You enjoy setting goals that are of a short-term nature and low risk. You will find that making a "to do list" is most beneficial. Trust can be an issue for you, it is an important gift to give someone. Your need for security, and low trust in unfamiliar circumstances, can be a performance block. Watch for the tendency to be hard on yourself and therefore, easily discouraged. It is important that you get 8 to 9 hours of sleep a night to reduce the effects of stress.

Communication tips:

When communicating with a person who is "S", be authentic , show sincerity, and allow trust to build. Listen carefully and give them the facts and assurances that they need. Slow down the pace of speech and be friendly. Do not try to control or dominate. Ask questions and allow time for response.

C stands for **Compliance:** Follows rules, precise and attentive to detail, exact, likes the facts vs. emotion, critical thinker, likes privacy, perfectionist, task-oriented, objective thinker.

If your score demonstrated a high number in the "C" column, you maintain high standards and are probably well disciplined. You will follow rules and procedures and are aware of the consequences of not following them. You are a critical thinker and strive to be precise and accurate. You enjoy collecting data and knowledge and you're willing to dig for it. You have a natural ability to organize and analyze as you develop systems. You are concerned with the effects of change in both your personal and professional life. You are good at setting safe goals probably in many areas. Use this workbook to calculate and plan a strategy to achieve the quality of life you want.

Your communication style is deliberate and non-emotional. It is doubtful that you will use gestures or facial expressions as you converse with people. You will ask the right questions so that you can get the right answers. You would prefer not to "fluff."

Coaching insight:

Your need for information and attention to detail assures that the project that you are engaged in will be of the highest quality possible. Sometimes, you may suffer "analysis paralysis" and question too much. Because you maintain such high standards, you may be too hard on yourself, and too critical of others. Strive for excellence and allow a mistake here and there. Remember that procedures and methods serve you, not vice versa. Learn to think outside of the box. Attempt to delegate and begin to verbalize your feelings with the people that you do trust. Show a little more enthusiasm when you converse. Your performance blocking fear is that your work will be criticized. An important stress reliever for you is alone time, you'll need to find a "cave" or retreat area in your home or office.

Communication tip:

When communicating with a person who is "C", be matter-of-fact unless invited to be personal. Your pace should be slow and deliberate. Do not waste their time. Give more information than you would like and make sure that you answer all questions. Follow through on promises and provide evidence for your conclusions. Use brochures with data, not hype. Give them time to make a decision and do not be pushy.

Now that you have a sense of how you behave and what your passions are, we can continue our coaching. The next section will reveal your dilemma, those inherent challenges you face. Knowledge will light your path.

DILEMMA

Your dilemma: Stuck between a skull and a soft place.

The impact that humankind has had on the physical world is remarkable. In the past 30 years the advances in technology, particularly as applied to information technology, have been staggering. When Neil Armstrong landed on the moon, the computer used to calculate the trip had an eight kilobyte memory capacity. Today one would be hard pressed to find even a hand held video game with such limited capacity. Our lives are much more complex, and yet, the qualities that are uniquely human are in more demand then ever.

According to new research, technical expertise is only half of what's required to be successful. Studies conducted by the University of Washington and the University of Michigan show that people who succeed in high tech, high stress jobs have common cognitive traits that enable them to thrive under pressure. Hard knowledge of technologies may be less important for those looking to rise to the top of their fields than "soft" skills—intuition, the ability to process a lot of information, and decisiveness.

"Specific technical know-how isn't as important as a good measure of emotional intelligence and intuition," says Jon Carter a recruiter at Egon Zehnder International in Palo Alto CA., "...the one's whose personal contributions save the company from disaster are those who bring grounded or factual intuition to bear on the job, people who can assimilate large amounts of data, in a very analytical way, and can synthesize it, and then step back and let their intuition kick in, can have what it takes to make it in technology ."

In his book, ***Emotional Intelligence,*** Daniel Goleman agrees that E.Q. (Emotional Quotient) is as important as I.Q. (Intelligence Quotient). While mathematics and linguistics measure I.Q., there also is a need to measure cognition, the combination of thoughts and feelings that constitutes your cognitive abilities.

In a moment, you will be taking another set of assessments that can measure and give you a customized approach to developing these important life skills.

If you want a better life, learn to make better decisions. Some of your decisions are, of course, pivotal life turning points, like marriage, having children, and career options. However, most of the decisions you face are of a much smaller magnitude, and yet, the sheer number can be overwhelming at times. The irony is that sometimes there are so many options, that you may actually feel as if you have no choice in the matter at all. Far too many people suffer from the disease "analysis paralysis," and are tortured by the "What if I... what if it's the wrong choice?" paranoia. This disease eventually erodes your confidence to the point that even the relatively insignificant decisions cause distress. Soon you avoid the big ones and tolerate life as you now know it.

The naked truth is that most of us tend to view and live our lives through our emotions rather than through logic, which creates distorted and inaccurate perceptions. The cost is staggering.

What you have experienced in your life is a result of the decisions and actions you have made, up to and including today. If you want the rest of your life to be different, learn to discern and develop the skill of *conscious decidedness.* Learn to distinguish what is *truly* important and how to prioritize your actions. Conscious decidedness is a rational approach that connects a reason along with a personal value. Every choice you make becomes a judgment call as to its relative importance to you. The power of choosing between things is meant to be an act of your free will. However, as we shall see, these strong irresistible impulses are greatly influenced by your past experiences and colorized, like an old film, by your emotions.

We all make decisions based on our reasons and values, yet most of the time, we are not fully conscious of the decision process. As an example, you could say, "I am going to exercise (choice) five days a week because (reason) I have gained too much weight and (value) I want to be healthier." You could just as easily have said, "I can't start exercising (choice) because (reason) I simply lack the will power to follow through and (value) I'm too tired to try."

Do you see the difference? Which one is rational? Which "you" do you want in charge?

BEFORE YOU CAN TRULY MOVE FORWARD IN YOUR LIFE, YOU MUST LEARN HOW TO TELL THE DIFFERENCE BETWEEN WHAT YOUR EMOTIONS ARE DICTATING, AND WHAT YOUR RATIONAL MIND IS PORTRAYING. If you fail to grasp this distinction, prepare to spend a lot of sleepless nights tossing and turning with a head full of questions and heart full of anxiety and guilt.

It is time to wake up and see the opportunities you are stepping over. Did you know that success is delivered at your doorstep, wrapped in layers of choices? That's right, at the very center of the decision process is the reward. You may not see it because your focus is on what you don't have, instead of what you want to attract into your life. "Frankly" speaking,

"How can you see anything when you're sucking on your thumb?" Look, I'm not trying to be hard on you. Honestly, I can relate to whining. There was a point in my life when I was discouraged, frustrated and worried, like many people. I was both "life-less" and "lifestyle challenged," or so I thought. One day my bride, Cathy, tiring of my whining, hung a ribbon around my neck with a baby pacifier attached. It was not the medal I had hoped for. To add salt to the wound she had me read aloud the following quote from Lewis Quimby, *"Whining is anger forced through a very small opening."* And yes, we are still married!

As we shall discover, fear and anger, along with an obsession to have life make you happy, stunt your natural growth. Fear and frustration had slowly blinded me. Kind of like the boiling frog. Everything is an obstacle when you lose sight of your vision. Great coaches ask painful and provocative questions and, like a great coach, my wife is relentless. She wanted to know what I was going to do about my situation. So I asked myself, "What does this mean to me?" and "What can I do about it?" The personal growth process that you are reading is a result of my labor pains and her courage to tell me the truth. A little like my wife, my role in your life is to stand beside you and hang the truth on you.

The truth is that every single day a gift is laid at your feet waiting to be opened. Get the pacifier out of the way so that you can see it. Tear into the package and claim your prize.

Have you ever watched a child at her birthday party? She can be overjoyed and overwhelmed at the same time because of the choices she must confront. First, she must choose which present to open. Will it be the closest, the biggest or the prettiest? Secondly, she must choose the best method to tear through the wrappings. As she shreds through the mound of gifts, she builds the efficiency of a factory assembly line worker, methodically dismantling the paper that stands between her and happiness. This book and process is your opportunity to claim the prize, so dive in with both hands, both feet and teeth, if necessary. CHOICES ARE GIFTS IN DISGUISE.

Did you know that not making a choice is, in fact, a decision? That's right, even when you are confused or stuck, you are deciding not to do something. So, there is no where to run, no where to hide. The only way to be happy and free is to be AT-CHOICE. Free to be who you are and free from the need to control the lives of others. Being who you are is your special reason for being alive. Knowing who you are and what you are here to do, is a self-discovery process that is directly connected to the choices you make and the actions you take. The only alternative to freedom is bondage. Casually observing or going with the flow is to be AT-RISK. In this state of mind, you are no longer in control of the day, let alone your life. Everything you do is either because of duty, obligation, or consequence. You will end up feeling like a dangling marionette, helplessly reacting to the whimsical commands of a puppeteer. Life then becomes a soap opera and each day is a brand new crisis or a droning portrayal of the day before, and the day before that.

The act of choosing gives you the authority to write your own story. Compose the next chapter of your life beginning with a scene where you sail off into the sunset, partner in hand, free to go where you want, whenever you want.

You have been designed to emerge victorious in the human race, not to suffer defeat in the rat race. Go ahead and jump off the treadmill before it's too late. The human race is much more humane (pun intended). Simply make an agreement with me THAT YOU WANT TO LIVE YOUR OWN LIFE AND NOT BE CONTROLLED BY ITS DRAMA. This is a powerful choice. The very moment you proclaim your freedom, vast resources are deposited in a success reservoir ready to be tapped. Your success reservoir will continue to grow exponentially with each positive thought, decision, and action you make because the universe will provide an equal contribution. Knowledge and awareness of how to make use of all this power will make all the difference in your life.

YOUR BRAIN IS THE FINAL FRONTIER

Where do your thoughts come from? What role do feelings and emotions play in your life? Should we control them like the half human, half Vulcan, Mr. Spock of " Star Trek" fame? We are going to search for these answers together as we explore the inner-universe between your ears. Our immersion into the inner-universe of emotions and mental processes is intended to illuminate your way so that you will achieve everything you want.

It is folly to even attempt the quest for a profound lifestyle without a practical knowledge of how your mind actually functions. The primary directive for your journey is for you to develop volitional abilities (deliberate, conscious and logical thoughts), giving you the power to choose freely. When you act of your own volition, you make decisions free of distortions and counterfeit purposes. When you can exercise your logic in any situation you are empowered to create the life and lifestyle you want.

I am not implying that you must become a non-feeling automaton to achieve success, as a matter of fact, the intent is to have you become even more conscious of your emotions so that you can enjoy a guilt-free life, and the fruits of your labor. EMOTIONS ARE, QUITE LITERALLY, A CHEMICAL ENERGY IN MOTION FOR WHICH YOU CAN DECIDE THE DIRECTION, WITH DISCIPLINE AND PRACTICE.

You were born with a powerful quantum machine called the brain. This gelatinous mass is your dream machine. It contains a staggering 100 billion neurons and is encased in a bony skull, floating in a pool of cerebrospinal fluid. The disturbing reality is that most of us never received an operational guide or the on-going tech support that we need. So, I think it would be a good idea to probe the "wet-ware" and see what we can discover. We are going to blend traditional wisdom along with the emerging *Bodymind* model, to help us navigate deep into your head to understand such a complex subject as you and your brain. Consider this your formal invitation to attend the following introductory lecture, B.Y.O.B. (Bring Your Own Brain).

The brain is the organ, the mind is its activities, the present, its product.

-"Frankly"speaking

There is remarkable research in the field of neurobiology that is creating fascinating models of how your brain works. Human kind's curiosity, coupled with the recent advances in medical imaging, has illuminated the shadowy recesses of the brain. Yet, the more we learn, the more questions we have. It's like the self-discovery process that you have embarked upon. Just when one riddle is solved, another one shows up. Research is pushing us back to the future, causing a profound shift in our understanding of how the body and mind function as one.

Dianne Connelly was the first to coin the word *Bodymind* to reflect the traditional Chinese medicine beliefs that **the body is inseparable from the mind.**

In her book, *Molecules of Emotion*, Candace Pert, Ph.D., defines our dilemma.:

"Emotions are at the nexus between matter and mind, going back and forth between the two and influencing both...thus it could be said that the traditional separation of mental processes, including emotions, from the body is no longer valid."

You experience the world through your bodily senses. These nerve impressions stimulate ancient emotional responses that are shared with every race and culture on this planet. While you are unique, you, nevertheless, remain a part of the collective family of humankind. Whether you are Italian, Native American, Asian, African American or Caucasian, you share a common emotional language. University of California professor, Paul Ekman, has confirmed Darwin's theory that **humankind has six basic emotions.** In this trans-cultural study, the participants were shown photographs of different people with a variety of facial expressions. The subjects were monitored with various instruments that would record their physiological responses to the pictures. The results were striking. He concluded that we not only read the emotional expressions of others, we actually react in a profound involuntary way. The six emotions are: **fear, anger, disgust, sadness, surprise, and happiness.**

Since cognition is a blending of feelings and thoughts, we must develop **emotional intelligence** if we are to take charge of our thoughts and direct them.

Our dialogue from this point forward will focus on the two emotions that cause us the greatest grief: fear and anger, as well as the seductive distraction called happiness. The "Triune brain" model (brainstem, limbic system, cerebral cortex), can help us get our arms around the challenge that our *Bodymind* "wiring" incites.

Don't Let Your "Rat Brain" Get You In a Trap!

In 1973, Paul MacLean, senior research scientist at the National Institute of Mental Health proposed that the brain is made up of three distinct subdivisions. He identified the brainstem, the limbic system and the cerebral cortex. The brainstem is the central part of the brain where it attaches to the spinal cord. It controls countless bodily functions, automatically. It is just like a thermostat, regulating a building. Imagine how difficult life would be if you had to consciously monitor and control your heartbeat, respiration, or temperature? This more primitive part of the brain is often called "the reptile brain" and was thought to be the source of our more basic urges. How about calling this part of us the **lizard brain**? Picture a lizard slithering along the ground, darting its tongue in and out, sensing the environment to detect danger, while searching for food and a date.

Wrapping around your brainstem is the limbic system. This important part of the brain is a conglomeration of many interconnected structures. It functions as the receiving center for all of your emotional triggers and controls their reflexive responses. All of these reactions occur well before you have had time to think about them. This second part of the brain is often referred to as the "mammalian brain." Let's call it the **rat brain** for fun's sake.

Sitting at the top, we have the third part of the model, the cerebral cortex. This is associated with our higher functions like logic and understanding, conscience and so on. We will call it the **sapient brain**. Through rigorous training and discipline, the sapient brain is able to suppress the powerful reflexes occurring in the lizard and rat brains. The activities that occur here separate you from the rest of the animal kingdom.

While dogs, cats, and chimpanzees are conscious beings, they do not contemplate the significance or consequence of being conscious. We are sentient beings who seek answers and significance. This is a blessing and a curse, as **we are the only beings in creation that interfere with their own growth.** Our design is perfect, it is our interpretation and discipline that could use some serious work. It is because of our emotions that we are moved to act. When understood and disciplined this "energy in motion" can be harnessed. In Latin it is described as "motus anima," meaning, "the spirit that moves us."

"Without the guidance of emotions, reasoning has neither principles nor power."

-Robert C. Solomon

It is when we confuse feelings with the activity of rational thinking that we get distorted versions of reality and this can cause great conflict and unnecessary stress. Our lives then become controlled by, rather than enhanced by, emotions.

Allow me to define the challenge that faces you in your quest for complete fulfillment and well being. The lizard brain and the rat brain exert an enormous influence in your daily activities. In fact, it is far greater than the impact the sapient brain has over them. This is why, in this book, you are encouraged to do a quantum plunge and create a whole new neural network by increasing your cognitive ability. In the   Peak Performance Process section under, "Mental Preparation," you will have specific instructions toward this goal. Every contact you have with the outside world is first monitored by this ancient alarm system. We are the products of thousands of years of inherited emotional reflexes. These reflexes are roughly twice as fast as the thinking part of our brains. Scientists estimate the time for an emotion to take place, after a given stimuli, is approximately twelve thousandths of a second (12/1000). The time for a logical thought to form is approximately twenty-four thousandths of a second (24/1000). In other words, we can't help but feel first, think second; feelings occur twice as fast. (Perhaps there is some merit in the old adage, "Count to ten").

The problem is that our minds and bodies have become hardwired for the same emotions our Paleolithic ancestors used to deal with their environments. Paleolithic man's environment was harsh and dangerous and he dealt with it accordingly. When he was threatened, his primitive instincts and emotional reactions were that of "fright and flight."

When he was threatened, his system automatically started squirting powerful performance enhancing chemicals into his blood stream. This elevated his blood pressure and prepared his muscles to fight or run. This, in turn, created a great deal of anxiety—it was also quite stressful. In fact, early man perceived everything in his environment as a stressor.

Today we still view our environment as stressful and we still have many of the same genes of early man. However, we no longer need these instincts and emotions to dictate our actions, nevertheless, they remain a part of us.

In the same manner as our ancestors, when we are challenged or frightened, we react in much the same way—through our emotions, which in turn releases epinephrine and nor-epinephrine into our systems, which in turn prepares us to fight or run (e.g., road rage, arguments, general anger, stress, anxiety, and fear).

Your body is an amazing machine. It is quite efficient. Once you react to a situation, thing or person by viewing it as a threat, your body immediately reacts with these fight or flight mechanisms. All of your body's energies are RE-ROUTED AND DIRECTED TOWARD THIS ACTION. Since your body has only so much energy at any given time, ALL OF YOUR OTHER FUNCTIONS SHUT DOWN during this time, including your mental faculties. Is it any wonder that repeated often enough, this stress reaction depletes your immune system and ultimately leads to sickness, disease and pre-mature death?

Most of modern man's ailments are self-imposed as a consequence of not understanding and disciplining emotions: diabetes, arthritis, high blood pressure, digestive problems, and cancer, to name but a few.

Fearless people die young. The purpose of fear is to protect you from a perceived threat. It is normal to be afraid of heights, high-speed chases, screeching tires, and lightening storms. This chemical energy in motion provokes a response that causes us to act, in order to establish a safe distance between danger and us. We unconsciously attempt to gain control by withdrawing, avoiding, or running away from the real or perceived threat.

In a scene from the prequel to "Star Wars," entitled "The Phantom Menace," the famous Jedi Knight Qui-Gon Jinn was asking permission from the counsel of Jedi Masters to train the young Anakin Skywalker. The head of the counsel, Yoda, remarked that there was too much fear in the young candidate. He warned, "Fear leads to anger, anger leads to hate, hate leads to suffering." His prophecy was correct as the adult Anakin Skywalker, father of Luke Skywalker, turned to the "dark side" and became the infamous Darth Vader.

Fear often creates a cascade of chemical alarms that disturbs the slumbering dragon of anger. Once it is fully awakened, it is nearly impossible to slay. The single mission of this dragon is to destroy and eliminate all perceived obstacles in its path. When we express these heated bursts of energy everyone gets burned, the person who is smitten, as well as the aggressor.

> *"Anger makes the blood around the heart boil."*
>
> -Aristotle

Wow! When you consider the devastating reality and health consequences of this statement, it is apparent that heart disease is preventable. Lifestyle choices have consequences and the decision to discipline your emotional reactions could save your life. Fear leads to suffering, whether it is turned inward upon yourself, or projected towards others.

Aggressive behavior is the obvious discharge of anger, yet the more subtle forms, like frustration or criticism, have the exact same effect on our *Bodymind* physiology. These suppressed angers can be felt as shame, guilt, resentment, and even depression. Depression is a serious mental health condition requiring professional intervention. Yet, we all have bouts of a more benign stage of this common imbalance, and, if recognized early, can be prevented. This quote sums it up nicely:

> *"Depression is anger without the enthusiasm."*
> -Anonymous

Feed it and it grows. If you choose to give into the emotions of fear and anger, your more primitive *lizard* and *rat* brains take over. A vehement explosion is uncontrollable once encouraged. Therefore, the part of your brain that you use for lucid reasoning, the *sapient brain,* completely shuts down. The rat attacks the trap because his survival instincts leave him no choice. In human beings, this condition is called "cognitive incapacitation," the literal translation is "unable to think or see straight." When you are upset, just like the rat, you are unable to think through and beyond your instincts. When you repeat any behavior, your brain establishes strong connections (the beginning of hard-wiring) that require a huge amount of conscious energy to break.

The only antidote to the bio-toxin of anger and unmanageable fear is relaxation. When we are relaxed, trusting, and logical, the lizard and rat brains sleep, and the sapient brain stretches and grows.

An exaggerated response to the ordinary events in your life promotes night and day-mares. Your natural inner *Bodymind* connectedness is splintered into emotional shards, because intense emotions create their own neural assemblies.

Whenever your *Bodymind ego-system* is imbalanced, you are vulnerable to the severe feelings of dread, despair, fright and terror. People who are anxious at any stage of this emotional kidnapping often complain that they are easily distracted from their daily routines and lack drive and focus. The result is a much different mindset than any normal, thoughtful state. You are unable to reflect on the past or speculate on the future. You are essentially trapped in the moment.

Experiencing the present is healthy and joyful, yet being imprisoned is a hopeless predicament. It is the same as a deer crossing the highway that becomes mesmerized, frozen in time, by the oncoming headlights of a big rig.

"Even if you're on the right track, if you just sit there you'll get run over."

-Will Rogers

The hell of it all is that until you are run over, you are essentially a "dead person walking," passively sensing the sights and sounds of the world around you. This unnatural survival energy eventually attracts into your life that which you fear most. If you are dreading bankruptcy and continue to feed the emotion, guess what happens? If you are jealous and fear that your significant other will cheat on you, guess what? If you are worrying about your health and fail to act, guess what?

Not all of our negative traits came from thousands of years of evolution though, some have been acquired more recently. These include the things we learn from our parents, school, church and our friends, in short—society. This could be ultra competitiveness, jealousy, hate or any number of negative emotions.

Sticks and stones may break my bones (they heal), but words will forever harm me. Words and offenses can be forgiven, but not forgotten. Recent research on childhood abuse victims confirms that this early exposure to stress generates molecular and neurobiological effects that alter neural development. Be careful of what you do or say when emotionally charged. Protect yourself and family from emotionally immature people. Do it now.

Some good books on you and your emotions are: *Emotional Intelligence*, by Daniel Goleman, *Adversity Quotient*, by Paul G. Stoltz, and *Brain Story*, by Susan Greenfield.

The only way you can avoid stress is to take a dirt nap. That's right, death is the only way to remove yourself from the stress of this world. Therefore, if this is not a part of your immediate plans, perhaps we can find a strategy to lessen its control over your *Bodymind*. This is another crucial truth for you to consider and apply to your life.

We have a great deal of insight about stress and its deleterious effects on our health as a result of the pioneering research by Dr. Hans Selye. In his book, *The Stress of Life*, he has identified our challenge and has inspired me to consider our options. We are going to make a distinction between stressors and stress. *Stressors* are situations, people, or things in our environment that we perceive as stressful. Stress is our response to the demands of these perceived forces. It is your natural *Bodymind* internal reactions. Stressors, for the most part, are changes in our external environment that demand adaptation from our internal environment. Therefore, stress is unavoidable. In fact, nature is designed to provoke responses in our *Bodymind*, and it is through our stress responses that we grow.

Stress causes our brains to continually grow new neural connections and this is how we form memories and learn to think. Consider this example, when a bone is fractured it is the stress of gravity pushing the two pieces together that causes the healing reaction. One more example from nature: There are certain species of pine tress that will only release their cones of propagation if they are stressed by the torrid flames of a forest fire. So, learn how to use stress to *grow* and release your legacy upon the world.

You have probably suspected that there is good stress and bad stress, and you are right again. Dr. Selye called "distress," the harmful or unpleasant variety. Failure or humiliation are examples of this kind of stress. Please remember that our emotions and our self-view color many of our judgments concerning success and failure. Therefore, a healthy self-view and balanced ego-system will determine the "eustress," which is the pleasant or curative form. A perfect example of this is the personal growth that you are experiencing as a consequence of your active participation throughout this book. You have chosen to stretch and grow from where you are to where you want to go.

Whenever you are engaged in exhilarating, creative work you are growing as a result of this form of stress. Every success that you celebrate causes an internal change called "eustress."

We come into this world with a finite Adaptive Energy Account. That means that we were born with the perfect amount of energy to cope and thrive in any natural environment. How natural is the life that you have created? If you knew exactly how much adaptive energy you had remaining, how would this effect your life choices?

We can, to some degree, measure this account. You have a biological age and a chronological age. The chronological age is the length of time you have been alive. The biological age is determined by how you have lived your life to date. We can predict that most people at a given age have a response to aging and by measuring a few indicators we can get a good picture of how they are doing. For example, spinal alignment, nerve function, muscle tension, heart and respiration rates, strength, flexibility and a variety of important blood chemistries tell your story, and by comparing it to others who are your chronological age, we can come up with a ratio. This is a simple way to determine if you are expending too much life force and going into energy debt.

Fatigue determines aging

How worn out have you become? Have you spent your adaptive account burning the candles at both ends, and the middle?

Your body's tissues don't lie! They tell your story without the "yeah buts." How is it that some people always look "so good for their age," while others look wrinkled and listless before their time? Are the young looking ones lucky and the unhealthy folks unlucky? Certainly, heredity contributes a share, **yet it's your choices that determine how well or poorly you age.**

The bad news is that ignorance of these matters is not bliss. It can be deadly to you and your vision. The good news is that your body can restore itself to an amazing extent with guidance and purposeful effort.

In my Chiropractic wellness practice, I listened to my patient's health history, the traumas, heredity and other events outside of their control. A health history is his/her story and, as a Doctor of Chiropractic, I focused on the health of the nervous system and the health habits of the person. By partnering with a concerned and knowledgeable doctor you will be held accountable and become inspired to form new behaviors or strengthen your healthy ones. Invest the time and the money to restore and maintain your health because you and your dreams are worth every dollar. Use the Physical Preparation part of your Peak Performance Process (to come later), with vigor and enthusiasm. Consider carefully the effects that your choices have on your destiny. Since you have the ability to take charge of many of your responses to stressors, implementing the Peak Performance Process will give you the edge when it comes to living long and prospering.

PART II

YOU ARE THE SUM OF YOUR RELATIONSHIPS

Re-la-tion-ship: *n*. A logical and natural association between two or more people or things.

Whether you know it or not, your life is lived through relationships.

There are three of them:

1. **Self-view:** Your relationship with yourself, of which, there are three interconnected parts:

Body-Your physicality and emotional agility.

Mind-Your mental capacity.

Spirit-Your sensitivity and concern with the nonmaterial values of Love and Truth.

2. **Other-view:** Your relationships with others. Valuing people through openness and acceptance.

3. **World-view:** Your relationship with the world, including money and possessions.

As we have already, we will continue throughout this book to discuss the role that emotions and perceptions play in all your relationships, as opposed to the use of logic, reasoning and understanding. GENERALLY, IN MOST PEOPLE, THERE IS SOME DEGREE OF DIFFERENCE BETWEEN WHO YOU PERCEIVE YOU ARE, AND HOW OTHERS SEE YOU. There is also a gap between how you see others and how you actually relate to them versus how you think you are relating to them (other -view). Then there is your relationship with money and possessions, perhaps the most emotional of your relationships (world-view).

Fulfillment comes from the complete engagement in the dance of life. Life is extraordinary; there are no ordinary moments, only lost chances to TAKE CHARGE of your life. YOUR TIME ON THIS PLANET IS MEANT TO BE A PERSONAL EXPRESSION OF YOUR ESSENCE (among other things). The world is waiting to be changed by your impact. It is through your PERSONAL PERFORMANCE that you find out what your essence is and then co-create and manifest your destiny. From this point forward, every experience, feeling, concern or dream is an opportunity to perform and fulfill your life. Regardless of how many books or seminars you have tried, they have all prepared you for right here, right now. Have you decided to give yourself one more shot at excellence? Life is a full contact sport. Life has a way of hurdling the dead and trampling the weak. It's time to get real.

"Men do not attract that which they want, but that which they are."

-James Allen

This simple statement is your key to a lifestyle of your design. The requirement is that you become more than you are at present, the complete, authentic you. Persistence in character development attracts opportunities and alliances. Living a life of virtue attracts wealth, materially and spiritually. Conversely, if what you are is a projection of fears and anger, then you will attract threatening events. If you are dishonest you will attract like, if you are controlling you will be controlled.

I have told you briefly that we were all designed to be perfect. I also referred to the three crucial relationships: your relationship with yourself, with others, and with the world through money and possessions. These natural, logical connections exist. All we need to do is understand how they work and STOP INTERFERING IN THIS RELATING PROCESS THROUGH OUR PERCEPTIONS AND UNSUBSTANTIATED FEELINGS.

I assure you that success and fulfillment are naturally occurring states of existence. In fact, you are already successful. If you haven't figured out how, then ask a very close friend to let you see your life through his eyes. Have him tell you what he thinks your gifts are.

Thoughts are like an echo reverberating in the world. What you send out returns, repeating the image over and over again. These thoughts affect matter because they are energy and that is why we are going to focus on your cognitive abilities throughout this book. You can OBTAIN a lifestyle and have what you desire and ATTAIN a life and BE who you were destined to become.

I want to be there when the person you are now meets the person you are destined to be!

RELATIONSHIP NO. 1
SELF-VIEW
YOUR RELATIONSHIP WITH YOURSELF

Congratulations, you are doing exceptional work! Hang in there, we are approaching an important mile marker. The most important vision you hold is the one of yourself. It is time to clear your SELF-VIEW. You know the saying, "The truth will set you free"? Well, the rest of it is "...and it can make you miserable at first." This is not a warning, it is a reminder that "clear thinking" is a different and powerful lens through which to view yourself and the world around you.

Discovering your hidden strengths and evaluating your soft spots is a lot like taking lessons in tennis or golf. You may feel so self-conscious that your "rat brain" reacts with a litany of fears. All of these responses are normal and, just like playing the games, once you learn how, you can kick back and enjoy it. Aim for where you are going and your innate intelligence and training will guide you.

In the following set of assessments, I will be holding up a mirror for you to gaze into. The reflection you see is, quite literally, your past, present and future all at once. You will see what was, perhaps, an innocent child-like grin. You will see the present, maybe stress lines or a twinkle of excitement in your eyes. And, you will see what is to come. Can you recall the scene in Charles Dickens' "Christmas Carol" in which Scrooge is visited on three consecutive nights by the ghost of Christmas past, the ghost of Christmas present and the ghost of Christmas future? Just like Scrooge, you can decide to change the outcome.

Your responses to these statements will help you design a program just for you. There will be no two journeys exactly alike. You may find that you have similar views with a few close friends, sometimes working with others and especially a coach/mentor will be a catalyst to this very natural process. Respond honestly. There are no wrong responses, only those that are right for you. When you answer these questions, please, be kind to yourself. Speak to yourself like you would one of your friends. As you begin, you may only see the shortcomings, the disappointments, the age spots or wrinkles. You may feel pessimistic, frustrated, angry or fearful. It will pass. Settle into this new you with a fresh view.

Before you answer these questions, take a few moments to clear your head, quiet your room, if possible, and take a few deep breaths. I want to introduce you to a very special person. After you have scored yourself, there will be a discussion of each of your answers and important coaching insights to apply immediately.

SELF-VIEW ASSESSMENT

Scoring Scale:
5=Always 4=Most of the time 3=Sometimes 2=Rarely 1=Never

(Circle one)
5 4 3 2 1 - I seek the approval of others.

5 4 3 2 1 - I find myself dwelling on the mistakes I have made.

5 4 3 2 1 - It's not my fault, things just seem to happen to me.

5 4 3 2 1 - While I'm sure that my parents meant well, some of my problems are a result of their influence.

5 4 3 2 1 - Details take the fun out of life.

5 4 3 2 1 - I'm not good at prioritizing. I get caught up in the little things.

5 4 3 2 1 - I rely on the opinions of others when making decisions.

5 4 3 2 1 - I have a difficult time taking action, even after I've gathered all of the information.

5 4 3 2 1 - If I really wanted to, I could be more successful.

5 4 3 2 1 - I am excessive when it comes to at least one of the following substances: tobacco, alcohol, prescription medicines, drugs, caffeine, sugar, chocolate, fast foods, television.

5 4 3 2 1 - I don't like quite. I leave the television on even if I'm not watching it, or I need to have the car stereo playing.

5 4 3 2 1 - I resist change or prefer doing things the way I've always done them.

5 4 3 2 1 - There never seems to be enough time to do what needs to be done.

5 4 3 2 1 - Setting goals just doesn't seem to work for me.

5 4 3 2 1 - When I reach a goal, I find it difficult to relax and celebrate.

5 4 3 2 1 - Sometimes I wonder if my dreams are really meant to happen.

5 4 3 2 1 - I feel tired and burned out a lot of the time.

5 4 3 2 1 - I feel like I'm just going through the motions.

5 4 3 2 1 - I'm not sure what I want anymore.

5 4 3 2 1 - Deep down, I believe that no matter what I do, things would just happen anyway.

5 4 3 2 1 - I feel like I have no real purpose.

5 4 3 2 1 - When I'm alone, I phone my friends to pass the time.

5 4 3 2 1 - I don't know what I want to do with the rest of my life.

5 4 3 2 1 - When I have a deadline to meet, I busy myself getting ready to do it vs. just doing it (e.g., instead of studying for the test, I clean out my desk).

5 4 3 2 1 - I should have a lot more money by this time in my life.

Add up your score:_____

SELF VIEW SCALE

25 - 50 Strong Self-View
Congratulations, you are no stranger to the self-discovery process. I invite you to use this book to confirm what you know and reach even higher.

51 – 75 Weak Self-View
You are certainly on the right path in your life. A few obstacles remain. Apply the COACHING INSIGHTS and watch these impediments disappear.

76-125 Poor Self-View
By now you realize what happens every time you get moving toward the life and lifestyle you want. Begin by acknowledging your courage to pick up another book. Accept the picture and messages you are receiving. Aspire to elevate your Self-view. You are in the right place at the right time. It isn't a coincidence that you are reading this book and coaching with me. It is our destiny. Thanks for letting me in.

COACHING INSIGHTS

1. *I Seek the approval of others.*

It is O.K. to seek the opinion of others, but an over-reliance on outside validation can erode your self-confidence.

COACHING INSIGHT: Separate your ideas and decisions from your emotional need to be liked and loved. If someone does not approve of your thoughts and ideas, they are not judging you, the person. Stop asking others the question "What do you think I should do?" and ask it of yourself.

2. *I find myself dwelling on the mistakes I have made.*

Blame and guilt are powerful emotional reactions to fear. An equally powerful antidote is forgiveness. Mistakes are natural and the more you attempt in life, the more mistakes you will make. Simply accept this reality and aspire to a better performance next time. Learn and don't repeat the same lesson. It is important to move away from the concept of right vs. wrong.

COACHING INSIGHT: You cannot focus on your success and your failures at the same time and move forward. The choice is yours. Read and implement Phase Three: Polish, of the Peak Performance Process.

3. *It is not my fault, things just seem to happen to me.*

While bad things do happen to good people, consider that some of your choices or inactions could be the source of your present suffering. In other words, the past does effect the present. Self-responsibility and self-accountability build character and attract good fortune.

COACHING INSIGHT: Stop being a victim. Changing your luck is as simple as being prepared and attracting different opportunities.

4. While I'm sure that my parents meant well, some of my ` problems are a result of their influence.

This is another example of avoiding self-responsibility by blaming others. Your parents probably did the best they could given their parenting skills and knowledge at the time. Know that it has helped to create who you are.

COACHING INSIGHT: Get over it, forgive them and move on. If these feelings of resentment still haunt you, pick up the telephone, give your parents a call and clear the slate. If your parents are deceased, visit their grave and have that forgiveness conversation posthumously. Your future is up to you, choose your course and take charge of your life, starting right now.

5. Details take the fun out of life.

Not everyone enjoys details and you don't have to be good at everything. However, following through by doing complete work is critical for success.

COACHING INSIGHT: Develop your strengths and, when possible, team up with someone who enjoys digging for information and enjoys details.

6. I'm not good at prioritizing. I get caught up in the little things.

When you begin this work, you may be overwhelmed with all the things you need to do. The reality is, you will need to expend a lot of effort catching up and attending to things you have simply let slide or ignored.

COACHING INSIGHT: Remember the order – self, spouse, immediate family, and career. Time management courses may be helpful. Read Stephen Covey's book, "The Seven Habits of Highly Effective People."

7. I rely on the opinions of others when making decisions.

It is important to have advisors and to consider different viewpoints. However, an over-reliance is often an attempt to shift the responsibilities of your actions to someone else.

COACHING INSIGHT: Develop resources, not dependence. You must trust your decisions and develop self-accountability and self-responsibility. The only way to become a better decision-maker is to make more decisions.

8. I have a difficult time taking action, even after I've gathered all of the information.

Analysis paralysis affects a large majority of people. Mistakes are an important part of your development.

COACHING INSIGHT: You will probably never have enough information to make the perfect decision. Very few decisions have life and death repercussions. The more decisions you make, the better you get and the more you trust yourself. Start to trust the other senses, those other than your feelings (i.e., sixth sense or intuition).

9. *If I really wanted to, I could be more successful.*

This could be another way of "rational-lying" and a sign that, at your core, you do not believe you have what it takes to succeed. Fear blocks us from setting the big goals because we risk failure.

COACHING INSIGHT: Work the Peak Performance Process with greater fervor and commit with every part of your being. Share your goals and aspirations with someone who believes in you and who is willing to hold you accountable.

10. *I am excessive when it comes to at least one of the following substances: tobacco, alcohol, prescription medicines, drugs, caffeine, sugar, chocolate, fast foods, television.*

Excessive use or abuse of these substances is a way to distract you from something. All of these chemicals alter your brain chemistry and if not disciplined can distort reality and suck the life out of you. Now the real challenge is, of course, dealing with any addictions. ADDICTIONS CONTROL YOU. The "acid test" for any suspected addiction is whether or not you can stop and stay stopped. There is no simple solution and most of the time recovery is a covering up vs. a resolution to the real problem.

COACHING INSIGHT: Begin with smaller habits, such as sugar or TV, and substitute other healthy activities. Serious addictions must be dealt with professionally. You won't hold onto things you OBTAIN and you will not be able to ATTAIN.

11. *I don't like quiet. I leave the television on even if I'm not watching it, or I need to have the car stereo playing.*

This could be a sign that you no longer want to think and want to be distracted from what is really going on in your life. Background noise fills a void but does not give you the silence you need to hear the voices of intuition. Another possibility is the challenge of the work home interface. We all enjoy being entertained and immersing ourselves in a mindless activity, however, if you are finding ways to *spend* time and not *invest* it, you are creating a growth deficit.

COACHING INSIGHT: Have a conversation with yourself whenever possible. That's right. Talk to yourself. It is an important relationship to develop. Take a voice recorder, journal or palm pilot to record your thoughts. Experiment with different strategies to leave work behind. Sit down and have a dialogue with your spouse and then your children.

12. *I resist change or prefer doing things the way I've always done them.*

At the core of all resistance is fear: being taken advantage of, being rejected, being criticized, abandonment, loss of security. Continue to do the things that are working. If they are not, you will need to change a behavior or procedure to get a different result. When businesses and people fail to adapt – they perish.

COACHING INSIGHT: Fears are a part of your *Bodymind* physiology. You cannot override them; seek to understand how they interfere with the goals you want. As you experience the fear, focus on what you are aiming to accomplish. Read the chapter on Change three times. You may start with little things like changing your hours, or where you sit at the dinner table. Take a different route to work. Ask yourself the question "How can I change my perception here and how will this benefit me?" This may enable you to take a different action.

13. *There never seems to be enough time to do what needs to be done.*

We have 1440 minutes a day. There are 60 minutes everyday that you are probably squandering. That's 365 hours a year. The work you are doing is also a process. It will always feel unfinished. Take it a day at a time.

COACHING INSIGHT: Identify distractions and create resolutions around them. Eliminate all seductive time wasters (e.g., TV, mindless chitchat or Internet chat rooms with no structure or outcome, busy work).

14. *Setting goals just doesn't seem to work for me.*

You may have set goals that never materialized and, therefore, you feel that it won't work this time either. Unless it is written down, it does not exist. Living without goals is like having a ship without a rudder, being continually blown off course and never setting foot on the promised land.

COACHING INSIGHT: Set two separate goals, one that is believable and one that is a complete pipe dream.

15. *When I reach a goal, I find it difficult to relax and celebrate.*

This is a sign of not enjoying the journey. If you are only thinking about tomorrow, you are missing the joy of the present moment.

COACHING INSIGHT: You are where you wanted to be. Be grateful for what it is you have, and for the people in your life, and, most importantly, for the heroic effort you have made. Keep the promises you have made with yourself. Take the time off or buy some small gift for yourself.

16. *Sometimes I wonder if my dreams are really meant to happen.*

Doubt is a normal emotion.
Courage = Doubt + Commitment + Action.

COACHING INSIGHT: Remember this, you would not have the dreams if they were not possible. Review the Thrival Principles and focus more effort in the Phase One, Spiritual Preparation of the Peak Performance Process.

17. *I feel tired and burned out a lot of the time.*

Burn out and de-motivation are common experiences. It happens to all of us at some point in our life for a variety of reasons. The point is not to stay stuck. Successful people simply get up one more time than they are knocked down. Most of the time, when we feel like a piece of burnt toast it is because we are not having any fun and we are not getting the results we had hoped for.

COACHING INSIGHT: Lighten up. When was the last time you took a real vacation? You will need at least 3 – 4 days off every six weeks to restore and recreate yourself. Take off wellness days, not sick days.

18. *I feel like I'm just going through the motions.*

You may not have identified your real passions, connected with the lifestyle you want to OBTAIN, or the life you want to ATTAIN. Review your Values Assessment, ("What do you value?") and follow the advice for 21 consecutive days.

COACHING INSIGHT: If money were no longer an issue, how would you spend your day? This will lead you to a greater connection with what you really want. Refer to the previous insight, take a break.

19. *I'm not sure what I want anymore.*

You have probably been frustrated by the efforts you have made in the past, compared to the results that you are experiencing. Let the answer come to you this time.

COACHING INSIGHT: Review the Values Assessment, ("What do you value?") and implement the recommendations. Take 3 days off to be alone in nature. Listen for your calling.

20. Deep down, I believe that no matter what I do, things would just happen anyway.

You may have slipped and assumed the role of life's spectator and forgotten what it is like to be a "player."

COACHING INSIGHT: You are a co-creator in your own destiny and your life is unfolding, even if you are passively participating. Decide to be a player one more time. Read the "Thrival Principles" thoroughly.

21. I feel like I have no real purpose.

People often mistake purpose for their mission, or their work in life.

COACHING INSIGHT: Your purpose is to develop all of your potentials and to seek a relationship with something greater than you. Don't die with your song inside of you.

22. When I am alone, I telephone my friends to pass the time.

We have conversations for different reasons, sometimes to pass on information or to report the activities of our day. Again, investing time vs. spending it makes sense, even with our friends.

COACHING INSIGHT: Invest a portion of your conversation as a dialogue that has a flow of meaning. Avoid contact with nay-sayers and whiners.

23. *I don't know what I want to do with the rest of my life.*

Why put so much pressure on yourself. You have the rest of your life to figure that out. You are never really off course.

COACHING INSIGHT: The first step is to sit down and figure out your personal, professional and other than you goals. See the "Planning your life" section under the Phase One: Mental Preparation, of the Peak Performance Process. Start with short-term goals.

24. *When I have a deadline to meet, I busy myself getting ready to do it vs. just doing it (e.g., instead of studying for the test, I clean out my desk).*

Busy work creates the illusion of momentum. This is one form of procrastination.

COACHING INSIGHT: Procrastination is not laziness – it is often a "veiled anger." Do you resent the activity, others, or yourself for having to do it?

25. *I should have a lot more money by this time in my life.*

This could be an indication that you are comparing yourself to other people. You may also have a preconception based on someone else's timetable for success.

COACHING INSIGHT: Read the chapter, on "Your relationship with money" at least three times. Let's start today and set a reasonable period for obtaining money.

Relax, we all have some work to do. I have observed that most people who take these assessments are hard on themselves at first. Lighten up, the good news is that self-awareness invokes a natural monitoring and correcting system.

Now, if you can pause for a moment, I urge you to go look at yourself in a mirror, a full length one if possible. I have found this exercise to be one of the hardest in the book and one of the most rewarding. Stare into and through the mirror until you can smile or giggle. For some of you that may take awhile. If you want to speed things up, get naked in front of the mirror and do ten vigorous jumping jacks. That's right get to know you from a whole different perspective. Go ahead make your day. Have some fun with this, and when you get back, I will be waiting. Whenever I start taking myself too seriously I do the "wild thing" in front of the mirror. So, feel free to do your dance, solo or in the company of fellow sojourners.

O.K., back to work. What did you see? Did you recognize the image? What do you like about you? What do you wish to improve? While visiting the Uffizi museum in Florence, I observed the meticulous process required to restore masterpieces to their original brilliance. Time and environmental factors had degraded the hues and fiber of the canvases of these valuable oil paintings. Technology and passion have made the restoration possible. The results are amazing. The colors are bright and the depth of the subject draws you into the painting. It is as if the artist just put the last stoke on the canvas. In fact, that is precisely what we are doing with you. We are using technology and passion to reclaim your brilliance and depth of perception. The tools and ideas in this book, along with the unleashing of the fire in your belly, make it all possible.

YOUR ENTIRE LIFE IS A RESTORATION OF YOUR ORIGINAL PERFECTION, THE PERFECT PORTRAIT PAINTED BY THE MASTER.

Your SELF-VIEW is a combination of SELF-ESTEEM and SELF-EFFICACY. It is your core belief about you. It is vital to your journey that you develop a healthy confidence and sense of deservedness. Knowing that, no matter what events happen, you will thrive in any environment. The self-assessments and the other actions you take in this book build you from above, down and then inside, out.

Let's talk a little bit about what SELF-ESTEEM is. It is a perception of worthiness, or lack thereof. On a scale of 1 to 10, with 10 being the high, how would you score your self–esteem? Record your score and highlight it for a future reference point,_____.

Your life is either empowered and guided by a robust SELF-VIEW, or restrained and mislead by an unsound one.

You have a right to *pursue* happiness. You have the right to be SELF-FULL, which means your *Bodymind* and spiritual needs are filled. This is not the same as selfish. I'll explain a little later.

People who possess a healthy balanced respect for themselves reach their goals much faster and with less effort than those with weak or inappropriate ones. Have you noticed that people who are already wealthy seem to have *better* financial "luck"? They seem to have the "Midas touch"— everything they touch turns to gold. Their self-talk is telling, and sounds something like this, "I made it happen and this is just one instance in a long procession of successes to come."

This is not arrogance, rather it is SELF-ACCEPTANCE. As your self-esteem grows, you begin to feel more attractive. You become a magnet, attracting positive people and opportunities. Stressful events and set backs are taken in stride.

A low self-esteem is characterized by blaming others, an inability to give or receive criticism, and an over reliance on external validation. That is, we become needy for support and take little responsibility for what has or is happening in our life. The prevailing attitude is low energy and high pessimism. Even when this person has a windfall or positive break in their lives, their inner dialogue (self-talk) goes something like this, "Someone else made it happen. It will never happen again. I was lucky this time."

Because you will be taking action on the things that are revealed to you in this book, your self-esteem will automatically rise, no matter how high or low it is.

SELF-EFFICACY is the strong internal belief that you CAN DO IT. On a scale of 1 to 10, with 10 being the high, how would you score your self- efficacy? Record your score and highlight it for a future reference point,___.

This internal knowing results from discipline and the courage to press on, in spite of fears and self doubt. A strong self-efficacy can never be weakened because it is your personal talent pool, your unique gifts that can never be taken away. This healthy confidence in your ability to learn, to think and make appropriate choices is your security. If you fail in one business venture, you simply take the knowledge you gained and move on without skipping a beat. In the Performance section of this book, we will outline how to buff your self-efficacy.

Watch out for these warning signs: People who suffer from low self-efficacy say things like, "If I really wanted to be more successful I could." or, "This is good enough. I'm doing better than most," or, "What is the minimum needed to get the job done?" These statements begin to poison us and interfere with our real selves. If allowed to build momentum, it becomes a pervasive feeling that, no matter what we do, we have no control over the outcome. The self-talk becomes, "I can't help it, that's just the way I am."

One way to increase certainty and confidence is to decide what your passion is and then determine which skills will be needed to master your passion. You can begin by examining what you've already accomplished and apply those habits to new endeavors.

If it is true that beauty is in the eye of the beholder, what happens if the beholder's vision has become fogged and his or her image distorted? Would what we see be a clear picture of who we are? Would our perception of others and ourselves be accurate? How would we view the events that are occurring right now? When we reflect on the things we have done, would our hindsight be 20/20, or could a distorted self-view interfere with our perception? As we gaze into the future, is the crystal ball clear, or can it have inclusions that distort the light?

Most of us suffer from a degree of self-view dis-ease. I define dis-ease as a state of distress and tension not yet a mental illness. This dis-ease causes a dysfunctional relationship to develop between you and you. Every effort and feedback you receive is seen through this mirror first. That is why we are looking for flaws in the mirror, not in you. This self-view could have become distorted by outside forces. (e.g., society, family, etc.) In our desires as children to fit in, we adjusted our attitudes and behavior to fit the views of the authority figures around us. The more successes and failures we had with these imposed views, the more they became an unconscious part of us.

What if, when you gazed into the mirror, you were seeing yourself through the perspective of your parents? You could then be unconsciously judging yourself according to their expectations and hopes for you, rather than your own. If you spent most of your life measuring yourself by this view, you would have had little time left to dream about what *you* want for your self.

For example, what if, as a youngster, a kind teacher told you that you were a gifted child? How would you have felt as you sat down to take your next test? What if, instead you had been mistakenly labeled as a slow learner or as having attention deficit? Would that attitude have shifted your focus? The obvious answer is most definitely. Remember, other's views can be true or false. They are just as susceptible to the same self-view disease that you are.

We act in accordance with what we perceive to be true. As a dramatic example of this, several years ago a woman in California, as reported in the Los Angeles Times, was diagnosed with an incurable form of cancer. Her doctor told her that she had only six months to live. Sure enough, six months later she died. Unfortunately, she did not have cancer, she had been incorrectly diagnosed. The power of the mind is truly awesome. What it perceives to be true, is true. How do you think the years of relentless visual and auditory experiences and opinions foisted on us by the media, have affected your views? How has that molded your view of reality? Truly knowing who you are, the real you, the essential you, and why you are here, outside the views of others, will give you peace of mind, and a profound sense of contentment and purpose.

It is quite evident that, to some extent, each of us is judging ourselves according to the values imposed upon us from the outside. Our internal responses, whether rebellion or compliance, determine how much stress and disease momentum we have gained.

(Note from your coach: Whether the things that are blocking you came from society, your family, evolution, your diet and exercise decisions, or all of the above, isn't that important. I am not here to psychoanalyze your past. As your surrogate coach, it is my job to deal with winners who want their "now" and their "futures" to be better. Just remember this: When you judge yourself through the prism of others, you should stop and remember that these "authorities" all possess inherent flaws as well as any good judgment).

A balanced ego-system

There is a plethora of information devoted to the topic of ego. It is the most important part of your self-view projection and, therefore, we must wrestle with this idea called ego. However, I must confess, that when I started my quest for success, any reference to ego caused me to feel guilty. Ego was something to be squashed or killed. Ego meant selfish and self-centered, and even as I started to break free from the rat race and the torture of mediocrity, I suffered guilt pangs. These growing pains were both real and imagined. Like most things, some of what I heard and much of what I understood was a distortion of the truth. Let's make an important distinction right here and now. Egocentric is the term that best describes selfishness. This individual sings the scale, DO, RE, ME-ME-ME. The loneliest people I have ever met are the most egocentric. Their attitude is that other people should fill their void.

Here is a healthy logical perspective. Ego as defined by Webster's, is: 1. The "I" or self of any person, thinking, feeling and conscious being. The conscious rational, able to distinguish itself from others. 2. The conscious rational component of psyche that experiences and reacts to the outside world (self-esteem, self-image).

This implies that without an ego we can not have any relationships, including the one we have with ourselves. In fact, our SELF-VIEW is shaped by all of the relationship experiences we are exposed to. Therefore, your ability to read these words and respond with thoughtful considerations and shifting feelings is brought to you by your sponsor—ego.

Humankind is sustained and interconnected through individual egos. "I" can without reservation tell "you" (ego to ego) that if being a conscious, rational and feeling human being is wrong, then I, for one, don't want to be right. What say you?

There are some fascinating ideas about our psyches that were proposed by Eric Berne in the 60's, called "Transactional Analysis." The relevance to your journey is that there appear to be three ego states that determine our external behavior and social interaction. Beginning with the CHILD we experience creativity, spontaneity and enjoyment. The PARENT commands, directs, prohibits, controls and nurtures. The ADULT is capable of sorting out information and makes logical decisions. It is my opinion that a BALANCED EGO-SYSTEM blends all three ego states when appropriate.

For example, we have spent time learning to distinguish between our emotional reactions and our logical decisions. We have asked that you discipline yourself and change inappropriate behaviors. We have also expressed a real sense of fun and adventure in dreaming with the imagination of a child. Self-awareness unfolds to reveal perfectly designed layers of extraordinary elegance. Here are some things you can do right away to enhance your own self-view.

Self-view enhancers

Your future can be molded and fashioned if you decide, today, to enhance the present, stretch and grow toward the future, and let the past fend for itself.

1. Become "Spoiled Ripe."

If you don't spoil you, who will? Just when you think you are pampered, go one step further. When someone suggests that you are spoiled, simply respond by saying, "Thanks for noticing." Sleep on silk or high quality cotton sheets. Buy aromatic soap. Buy great hair products. Pay for DSL internet service. Upgrade your computer. Plan a mini vacation every 6 weeks.

Celebrate your accomplishments as they occur. If you have promised yourself a treat when you hit a milestone, then reward yourself. It's not a good thing to lie to your innate intelligence. Reward yourself with small luxury items. It's far better to give yourself small rewards along the way than it is to add expensive liabilities, such as a new car. How about a new jacket, or a day at the spa?

2. Tolerate nothing.

Make a list of the top 10 things in your life that consistently irritate you. As an example, a rattle in your car, a window that leaks, a stain on your carpet, a door that squeaks, a computer that is too slow, etc. Whether you know it or not, these things are on your mind taking up valuable space.

1.

2.

3.

4.

5.

6.

7.

8.

9.

10.

Now, begin to eliminate these irritations. Are they perceived or are they real? In other words, take the time to carefully examine what it is that irritates you and why. Perhaps you can eliminate some things just by thinking about them differently. Look carefully at each irritation. Are you responding to something from an emotional level, therefore, making it an irritation? If so, begin to use logic when confronted with this situation.

3. No Whining. No Complaining. No Blaming.

"A man's weakness and strength, purity and impurity are his own, and not another man's. They are brought about by himself and not by another, and they can only be altered by himself, never by another."

-James Allen

The minute you begin this plan, you are doing something positive and tangible toward your goals and toward becoming who you truly are. In essence, you are living the good life, to some degree, just by taking the first few steps. You are feeding the positive. When you feed the negative emotions, you build a momentum away from your dreams. Whining, complaining and blaming are all negative activities to build momentum away from your authentic, thriving self.

When someone asks you how you feel and you begin a long diatribe about the suffering and the wrongs heaped upon you, or just how miserable you are, you might as well be throwing gasoline on a fire. VERBALIZING NEGATIVE THOUGHTS ONLY BUILDS THEM UP AND MAKES THEM MORE REAL.

Change the subject. Reflect upon the good parts of your life and discuss those, even if, for that one day, your life isn't filled with happiness, choose to talk about what *is* good with your world, no matter how small.

Blaming is another negative emotion. You cannot have mature relationships with people if you habitually blame others for your plight. You cannot trust that you are destined to be successful if you complain. You will never build a healthy self-view if you blame yourself, either. Look for reasons, not excuses. You may have to begin with small things. Just accept that the room is too cold or too hot, without complaining. The drone of whining is hypnotic. Avoid people who are constantly complaining. If you are on the path to total fulfillment and peace of mind, you have no time "to major in the minors."

Take a TIME OUT right now and resolve to follow this mantra on a daily basis:

Today, I will not complain.

Today, I will not blame others or myself.

Today, I will not whine.

Today, I will not gossip about anyone.

Today, I will not speak negatively about anyone or anything.

I choose today, to say only good things about other people.

Make a promise that you will follow these five commandments for 30 days and you will be amazed at how easy this becomes and just how good you begin to feel. Before the 30 days are up, I guarantee you will be "catching" yourself in mid-sentence and changing the subject before you complain or blame. After 30 days, you'll wonder why you ever lived any differently. Once you begin to speak aloud positively and/or talk to yourself silently, it becomes easier to think positively. Little things add up and suddenly, you feel empowered.

RELATIONSHIP NO. 2
PEOPLE-VIEW
YOUR RELATIONSHIPS WITH OTHERS

There are over six billion human beings on this planet. Everywhere you go, you are confronted with the undeniable reality that people are part of the fabric of your life. Your attitudes concerning your fellow human beings will be one of the major determining factors as to whether your goals will be realized. Adjust your attitude to view humanity as DIFFERENT BUT EQUAL and you will establish a strong foundation for developing powerful communication skills. These skills and new perceptions will guarantee success in any endeavor you choose. Your self-view determines your perception not only of yourself, but how you see yourself in comparison with others. You have three choices before you. You can feel superior to others, inferior, or different but equal. You will discover that your perception varies widely depending upon whom you're interacting with and in what social context. You may cast a superior attitude toward a homeless person or someone who is immoral in your eyes. When you are meeting a person who, in your judgment, "has arrived," you may experience a feeling that in some way you are not as good as they are. This is a dilemma because it is our fears and other emotions that begin to cloud our judgment and cause stress and conflict. It is the *perception* of inequality that disrupts momentum.

It is time for you to look at the second relationship that determines how successful you will become, your relationship with others. In this section, you will be taking another assessment to determine how well or poorly you relate to others around you. Life skills include your openness, acceptance, and valuing of others, along with your ability to influence them.

INTERPERSONAL RELATIONSHIP ASSESSMENT

Scoring Scale:
5=Always 4=Most of the time 3=Sometimes 2=Rarely 1=Never

(Circle One)
5 4 3 2 1 - I have a tendency to interrupt people.

5 4 3 2 1 - When things go wrong at work, it's usually because someone else has dropped the ball.

5 4 3 2 1 - I have a tendency to hold a grudge.

5 4 3 2 1 - I have to keep my guard up or else someone will take advantage of me.

5 4 3 2 1 - Some people just know how to push my buttons.

5 4 3 2 1 - I would rather do it myself than have to fix the mistakes of others.

5 4 3 2 1 - I'm often accused of being moody.

5 4 3 2 1 - Most people are boring to talk to. They have much to say about nothing.

5 4 3 2 1 - I am a master at tuning in and out of a conversation and never missing a thing.

5 4 3 2 1 - I have found clever ways to make people think I'm listening.

5 4 3 2 1 - Some people just talk too slow, it's easier if I finish their sentences.

5 4 3 2 1 - When someone says something I disagree with, I want to jump right in and tell them my viewpoint.

5 4 3 2 1 - Too many people "fly by the seat of their pants."

5 4 3 2 1 - Some people waste so much energy talking.

5 4 3 2 1 - I could get a lot more work done if I could be left alone.

5 4 3 2 1 - I resent being told what and how to do something by my boss. After all, I know what my job is.

5 4 3 2 1 - There is at least one person that I dread bumping into.

5 4 3 2 1 - If I don't take control, nothing gets done.

5 4 3 2 1 - I find it hard to say what I'm feeling.

5 4 3 2 1 - Rules and procedures are to be followed.

5 4 3 2 1 - I don't care what others think of me.

5 4 3 2 1 - Only a few people really understand who I am.

5 4 3 2 1 - The only way to get some people to move is to put the "fear of God" into them.

5 4 3 2 1 - People take much of what I say the wrong way.

5 4 3 2 1 - People think that I'm too pushy, but I think I'm too intense for them.

Add up your score:_____

Other–view scale

25-50 Strong Interpersonal Skills
Well done. It is obvious that you have taken your natural abilities to connect with people and enhanced them. It is time for you to teach others.

56-75 Fair Interpersonal Skills
You are on track. It is likely that as your Self-view strengthens your acceptance and appreciation of others will improve. Study the Coaching Insights and seek to understand them.

76-125 Weak Interpersonal Skills
You have natural abilities, it's time to uncork them. Much of
the stress and conflict you experience is no longer necessary.
Learn to understand and love unconditionally and you will
receive the same in return.

COACHING INSIGHTS

1. *I have a tendency to interrupt people.*

This could be a sign of poor listening skills. You may be
focusing on your agenda and missing key points in the
conversations. It's also impolite and discourteous.

COACHING INSIGHT: If you scored a High "D" on your
behavioral assessment, take note to discipline this tendency to
get the results you want. Remember, people speak at 150
words per minute but we can hear 500 words per minute.
The void is excruciating at times, take a few breaths, it's not
really an eternity.

2. *When things go wrong at work, it's usually because someone else has dropped the ball.*

We all have a tendency to look outside ourselves for the
problem, blaming others for the things that go wrong in your
life. If you keep indulging this habit, you will miss a growth
opportunity.

COACHING INSIGHT: Accepting your responsibility does
not mean shifting the blame to you. Stop, have a dialogue with

your fellow team-members and come to a resolution. There is a logical solution to every problem.

3. I have a tendency to hold a grudge.

If you are among more than 40% of the population that has the behavioral style described as steady, methodical, systematic, relaxed, reliable, and adaptable you have a stronger tendency to hold a grudge when wronged (High S).

COACHING INSIGHT: Holding onto the past costs you, emotionally, physically and spiritually, robbing you of the stamina you need to OBTAIN or ATTAIN your desires. Today, not tomorrow, declare that you forgive those whom have hurt you or whose actions caused mistrust. FORGETTING WILL COME LATER.

4. I have to keep my guard up or else someone will take advantage of me.

You may have legitimate reasons not to trust people based upon your past experiences. Trust is both earned and given.

COACHING INSIGHT: Trust can be earned from making and keeping small agreements. Acknowledge these and then, most of all, learn to trust yourself. The reality is, your path involves people.

5. *Some people just know how to push my buttons.*

This may be just an example of giving control up. It is not what THEY do, but what YOU do with the information or action.

COACHING INSIGHT: The buttons are there because you have put them there. Review Part I, Dilemma: Stuck between a skull and a soft place, and work every step in Part III, Phase One: Physical Preparation.

6. *I would rather do it myself than have to fix the mistakes of others.*

This usually is an indication that there is a problem with the system or you may have a control issue.

COACHING INSIGHT: Do not blame the person. Try to set up a feedback loop that will take care of these mistakes automatically. One of two scenarios is likely occurring. The first is that you may have over-delegated and under trained. Second, you may have unrealistic expectations and demand perfection vs. excellence. Mistakes are normal. Even I make them (this is your cue to laugh).

7. *I'm often accused of being moody.*

This is either because you are susceptible to mood swings or you don't feel comfortable verbalizing. Sometimes the High "S" style is judged as being moody because they may not express as much enthusiasm as the High "D" and High "I" styles.

COACHING INSIGHT: Be aware of the things you may be doing that will affect the chemistry of your body like diet, alcohol and caffeine. Other factors may be improper lighting, lack of energy, lack of sleep. Review the communication tips in the How do you behave? (self-assessment section).

8. *Most people are boring to talk to. They have much to say about nothing.*

The lost art of dialogue permeates all of our relationships. Rather than judge the person, look for opportunities to bring meaning into the conversation. Some people have a tendency to report trivia and may have a fear to contribute their opinions. If you ask people for their opinions, don't criticize them. Take issue with the idea, if warranted (try to influence rather than control).

COACHING INSIGHT: Be patient with those who are important in your life. Draw them out by asking questions. Review the How do you behave? (self-assessment section) and communication tips. It will help to understand the behavior of others.

9. *I am a master at tuning in and out of a conversation and never missing a thing.*

Busted! I'm sure you may think that this statement is true. The reality may shock you. Dialogue is attentive, active listening with a congruent body language.

COACHING INSIGHT: Try focusing your complete attention the next time you are with someone. You will notice a flow of meaning that will surprise you.

10. I have found clever ways to make people think I'm listening.

Listening is more than eye contact, head nodding, and an occasional, "uh huh." You have mastered the art of deception, not connection.

 COACHING INSIGHT: Stay in the moment and you will find that it takes a lot less effort to be with people. Be genuine with people. If you don't want to listen, excuse yourself and leave.

11. Some people just talk too slow, it's easier if I finish their sentences.

This is an easy habit to develop and a very difficult one to break. Many times you are correct when you fill in the void, however, this is a sign of poor listening skills and A TENDENCY TO CONTROL OTHERS.

COACHING INSIGHT: Most people speak at the rate of 150 words per minute. The challenge is that we can accept words at the rate of 500 words per minute. Therefore, everybody talks too slow and we try to fill in the vacuum. Dialogue requires that you listen while the other person is talking. IF YOU ARE PREPARING A RESPONSE, you have stopped listening at that very moment.

12. *When someone says something I disagree with, I want to jump right in and tell him or her my viewpoint.*

Real conversations are an opportunity to expand your world and add to your knowledge and perspective. Dialogue is not debating.

COACHING INSIGHT: The moment you hear something you disagree with, focus even harder on what is being said in-between the lines. You don't have to embrace their view, you would be wise to value the person stating it.

13. *Too many people "fly by the seat of their pants."*

While it may be true that some people lack preparation and follow through, your perception could be clouded. If you have a Low "I" style, you may judge someone who is High "I" as too loose. Look at your score under the "I" section of the "How do you behave?" self-assessment section.

COACHING INSIGHT: Don't let your perceptions or feelings cause you to be too critical. Ask yourself, "What could I learn from this cavalier, nonchalant attitude?"

14. *Some people waste so much energy talking.*

If you are not a talker, you may assume that people who enjoy verbalizing could be doing something more meaningful. You may even consider silence golden.

COACHING INSIGHT: High "I" styles have a need to talk. It's that simple. People are different but equal, whenever you judge a person you create conflict and stress.

15. *I could get a lot more work done if I could be left alone.*

Interruptions certainly take us out of flow and can frustrate us. Watch for the tendency to put tasks over people.

COACHING INSIGHT: If you know that a critical task requires your undivided attention, then find a secluded area. You may have to set some boundaries with co-workers.

16. *I resent being told what and how to do something by my boss. After all, I know what my job is.*

Most of us do not like to be criticized and, unfortunately, few people are skilled at course correcting statements.

COACHING INSIGHT: Be cautious that you do not mis-interpret criticism of your work as a personal attack. In business there is a concept called structural authority. This "authority" gives your boss the privilege and right to direct your actions while at work. So long as they do not use this power as emotional authority then you are bound to follow.

17. *There is at least one person that I dread bumping into.*

Relationships can be another form of incompletions. Conflict and stress in relationship can create the greatest drain to your vitality. You can never have peace or freedom.

COACHING INSIGHT: Forgive yourself for the harm you may have done and forgive the harm done to you. Write a letter (you may choose to send it or not), make a phone call. Remember to forgive now, forget later.

18. If I don't take control, nothing gets done.

While you are incredibly gifted and may be able to do the job better than most, failing to delegate and develop the abilities of others severely limits your capacity to achieve. Also, learn to recognize when your communication skills are a major part of the problem. Are you saying what you mean to say? COACHING INSIGHT: Trust, delegate, inform, train, and then inspect what you expect.

19. I find it hard to say what I'm feeling.

Not everyone is comfortable with verbalizing, yet silence may cause others to feel that you are hiding something.

COACHING INSIGHT: Try writing down your thoughts and feelings. This practice may allow you to gain a confidence in verbalizing. Begin by doing this with people you trust.

20. Rules and procedures are to be followed.

For those of you who express the behavioral style that can be described as: meticulous, analytical, careful and precise, then you are motivated to comply. The majority of the population, however, does not share your view.

116

however, does not share your view.

COACHING INSIGHT: Your attention to detail and quality is an important asset to any team. Some rules may no longer apply in your life. Seek others who think outside of the box to gain a different perspective.

21. *I don't care what others think of me.*

There is a big difference between needing approval and caring about what others think. It is healthy to have a strong enough self-view that you are not hampered by needing approval. Yet, a strong response in this area could indicate that you think you are better than everyone else.

COACHING INSIGHT: As a human being, you need love and respect. Strive for a balanced ego-system. Love someone unconditionally and it will return to you.

22. *Only a few people really understand who I am.*

There are four major behavioral styles and within these are many different combinations. Learn to understand and appreciate different styles of people and you will probably get the same in return.

COACHING INSIGHT: Seek others with like interests. Refer to the self-view assessments under the "What do you value?" section and find others who share your same Values (e.g., If you are high theoretical find others who love to learn).

23. ***The only way to get some people to move is to put the "fear of God" into them.***

There are three ways to motivate others: fear (punishment), incentive (reward), or causal (investment). The least effective is fear.

COACHING INSIGHT: Control, as a strategy, has worked for you and has cost you. Attract people to your cause and mission.

24. ***People take much of what I say the wrong way.***

This, likely, is a result of your listening skills and dialogue prowess.

COACHING INSIGHT: Study and implement the communication strategies for all behavioral styles.

25. ***People think that I'm too pushy, but I think I'm too intense for them.***

This may hint at an over-extension of a behavioral style described as: demanding, confronting, direct and commanding (High D). You may find that you are impatient because you need bottom line results.

COACHING INSIGHT: 72% of the population has a slower pace; the job will get done. You may find that you get better results if you delegate and make sure that you have thoroughly instructed. People show their intensity and commitment in different ways than you do.

The ability to inspire cooperation in others catapults you ahead of the pack of mediocrity. People are attracted to good speakers and good listeners. Whenever I observe two people of equal talent and passion compete, my money is always on the one who has the better communication skills. Note that I said the best communicator and not the best talker. Communication combines exceptional listening skills along with the right cadence and tone of your speech patterns. Trust me, your communication prowess can be unleashed because it already lies dormant, covered by various wrappings of fear. These myriad fears have you wrapped up as tight as an Egyptian mummy, binding you to the realm of silent frustration.

Regardless of what business you are engaged in, it is personal because people are involved—everything in life is personal. Look at the "How do you behave"? section in Part I and study the communication tips.

Your personal and professional successes are either limited or expanded by your ability and desire to develop healthy egalitarian relationships. It is natural to have healthy relationships and, yet, it is not normal. We have a natural ability to connect and to communicate through language, physical expression and spiritual connection with others. When I say that it is not normal, I mean that most people interfere with this natural connective flow between people and, therefore, this has become the accepted norm.

The unfortunate consequence of miscommunication is emotional suffering. We have come to believe that conflict and stress in relationships are normal and acceptable. It is no wonder we submit to the inevitable and expect to breed dysfunctional families, broken homes and to fill divorce courts. In our society these events may be "normal" because it has become too common of an experience, however, it is not the "natural" order of conscious, balanced individuals. Life skills include great people skills. Understanding your behavior and having a sincere interest in understanding and appreciating other's behavior is a very solid foundation for success with less conflict and stress. Develop a keen awareness and adapt your behavior to meet people where they are. All worthwhile endeavors require people to harness their collective energies. Truly successful people promote their ideas and inspire others to join with them for a common good.

The ability to motivate others involves the art of dialogue, the ability to communicate your messages, and the ability to connect, *Bodymind* and spirit. THROUGH OUR INTERPERSONAL RELATIONSHIPS WE HAVE THE BEST OPPORTUNITY TO GIVE OUR LIVES AND THE LIVES OF OTHER'S, MEANING. If you are looking for "meaning" in your life, begin by contributing your energies to others first. It's the quickest route to fulfillment. We must see all people as equal but different, any other approach creates conflict and stress.

We are more alike than different.

When you look in the mirror, do you see your mom, dad or another relative? We all use expressions like, "She has my nose."or "He has my eyes. " or, "He is the spitting image of his father," as natural confirmations that we are more alike than different. We have two eyes, two ears, two lips, two arms, two legs, two lungs, one brain, one heart and an essence or spirit. HOWEVER, WE HAVE, UNFORTUNATELY, LEARNED TO

FOCUS ON OUR DIFFERENCES AND TAKING THIS POSITION TEMPTS US TO JUDGE, DISCRIMINATE AND EVEN DESPISE PEOPLE WE BARELY KNOW OR DON'T EVEN KNOW AT ALL.

Why have we become so obsessed with judging fellow human beings who demonstrate even the slightest variations from what we have come to believe is normal? Yes, we do have different cultural heritages, languages, physical attributes, attitudes, beliefs and passions. THIS DIVERSITY TEACHES US ABOUT OUR PURPOSE AND WHO WE ARE.

Loose the attitude of superiority and gain the respect, love and cooperation that you would like to receive.

I have an unusual habit that I want to share with you. When I am in the company of someone who is wearing sunglasses or prescription lenses, I ask permission to put them on my face. I am not sure where this quirky behavior originated, but I do know I enjoy it. I find it fascinating to look at the world through their lenses. Sometimes, I make a playful comment while pointing to myself and say, "This is how you could look." Moans are the usual response. While this exercise may not be a profound connecting experience, it is a bond, nonetheless. WHEN WE LOOK AT THE WORLD THROUGH THE EYES OF ANOTHER, WE DON'T HAVE TO WALK A MILE IN HIS SHOES.

Your attitudes toward your spouse, children, boss, co-workers and employees will determine whether stress and conflict stops the flow of abundance, or whether compassion and respect opens the flow gates. It is your choice. If you choose to live your life by judging yourself and others, stress and conflict will be a normal event. You will experience disharmony, fear, anxiety and frustration in all of your endeavors. However, if you choose to accept, respect and find value within yourself and each person, you will experience being loved. You will attain harmony and freedom and attract opportunities beyond your imagination.

Financial investments can produce huge returns because of compounded interest. Likewise, by fully investing yourself in others, you will discover that one (human being) plus one (human being) does not merely equal two. It produces exponential empowerment for both.

When was the last time you had a thought provoking conversation? Today, and everyday, endeavor to have at least one stimulating conversation. By dialogue I do not mean small talk, of the "How-about-those-Yankees" variety. See the good in someone and ask him what is new in his life. Listen with sincerity. If you have an opinion, ASK IF YOU CAN OFFER IT.

We have lost the art of conversation and the passing of ideas mouth to mouth. It's little wonder that people listen to talk radio. Go to the source and connect with a live thinking human being. Dialogues are literally a flow or streaming of meaning between people. Get to know people around you, the person at the office you never talk to or the mail carrier you don't pay attention to. Bring people out of the shadows of your own mind and into the light of day. Many will emerge from the darkness with depth and rich textures. We cheat ourselves by not getting to know the people we work with and live near. Don't wait until they die to learn how they lived.

It is also important to remember that when you STOP talking to others over an issue or conflict, you eliminate your options and there is nothing quite so depressing in life as not having any choices.

When you do not speak up, you disconnect. Much of the rudeness and insensitive things we see going on around us are happening because people have disconnected from one another. Invoke the "greater you" and be aware. Walk a mile in the other person's shoes. If you feel you are right and they are wrong, then state your case using logic, not emotion.

"Hate the sin and love the sinner."

-Mohandas K. Gandhi

Disagree with the behavior, not the person. Use diplomacy and truly listen to the other side. If another person is dealing from emotion, point that out and always remember, you can walk away, you have choices. Your rational mind discerns between right and wrong, night and day, good and evil. Being judgmental indicts the person or group. It is a lack of love, loss of respect, and below your nature.

SETTING BOUNDARIES

"Oh how I regret that I can't devote my entire life to you and your problems."

-Ashleigh Brilliant

Oddly enough, though good people skills are necessary, it is also imperative that you SET BOUNDARIES with some of the people in your life. That includes parents, siblings, spouse, children, friends, employers, and colleagues. A BOUNDARY is the behavior you DEMAND of others. Some examples might be a no smoking rule in your home, curfews, no screaming at me, no foul jokes in my presence, no whining and playing the victim. When you set a boundary with someone you are protecting yourself from harmful or hurtful behavior. This boundary helps define who you are to others. It protects you from harmful behavior and ATTRACTS THE BEHAVIOR YOU PREFER. Here are some examples: When the office story teller insists on telling you his latest off-color joke, simply say, "I appreciate you including me in your life. However, I am a modest person who is offended by crude jokes." Or, in the case of someone who expresses compulsion or addiction, your boundary statement is, "I will stand by your side if you get into a program and work it out." Or, when someone lights up, you can say, "I really don't want to smoke that cigarette with you." And, of course, there is the all too common parent/child scenario, "I am an adult, please don't treat me as if I am still a child."

Boundaries also ATTRACT the kind of behavior you WANT from others. Most people, if they respect you, will comply with your wishes. Yet, some will keep testing the wall to see if you are serious this time (children do this a lot). Remember, NO means NO. If it is translated as MAYBE or SOMETIMES, you will be responsible for whatever you have foisted on yourself. When a BOUNDARY is continually breached, you must move away, mind and body, at least temporarily. You can ill afford to waste energy defending your decisions and activities while you are moving your life forward and upward.

Remember, change affects people emotionally and, therefore, the "rat brain" can dominate for a time. Maintain your "sapient" approach, not as parent to child, but rather as the logical adult.

Some friends and family members will be fearful as they misconstrue the intentions of your efforts to change you from the inside out, as a judgment concerning them. At first, they may not be comfortable with your metamorphosis, but when they begin to recognize your courage and commitment, they may actually ask for your mentoring. Give them time to adjust to the new you.

When people tell you that you have changed simply say, "Thanks for noticing." Don't get caught up in their perception that you are somehow trying to be better than them.

Mediocrity loves company. Limit your contact with people who may pull you back into mediocrity. YOU ARE ON A MISSION, the most important mission of your life. In the sport of mountain climbing they use a term, "bagging", in reference to any fellow climbers who are not physically or mentally able to continue the assault on the summit. This individual is zipped up in his mummy bag and secured to the mountain. The idea is to eliminate the dead weight temporarily and pick him up on the return trip.

As you begin to work the plan, you will have to make these kinds of difficult decisions as well. You know who these people are, so limit your contact, at least until you've worked your plan.

> *"What's love got to do with it?"*
>
> -Tina Turner

No discussion concerning relationships would be complete without some reference to the "significant other" in your life. As I walk through the aisles of any bookstore I am reminded of how much and how little we know about discovering and nurturing monogamous relationships.

Love has different meanings for each of us. I would like you to consider these thoughts and add what you like to your present understanding. I view love as a pure spiritual quality that is then expressed through our *Bodymind*. The Ancient Greek language contains three separate words to draw a profound distinction.

Agape is unconditional love, non-judgmental, accepting and has no need for reward.

Philos is the "brotherly or sisterly" love we express to friends and relatives. As an example, the name for the city Philadelphia is derived from this word and is translated as "the city of brotherly love."

Eros is the term to describe the physical love and passion we have toward a very special friend, husband, wife, or life partner.

Therefore, if this pure love is expressed through our *Bodymind*, then it is susceptible to the lens of perception colored by our self-view and the strong pull from emotions. Love can feel happiness or sadness. It can be fearful and, therefore, controlling. Love not returned can become angry. How do you express love when your self-esteem has taken a hit?

The stark reality is that many relationships and marriages are not based on the principle of love at all, but rather "the feeling of being in love." Love means, "I love you as you are." This is in sharp contrast to the emotional feeling that pulls us from choice into chance. Being in love is like an e-mail (e-motion) with an attachment to your past and a wish for your future. As with e-mail attachments, you risk catching a destructive virus. The message carries memories of past heartaches and a hope of changing those cute little quirks once you are married. When these feelings wear off and your expectations have not materialized there can be trouble in paradise and someone can be cast out physically or emotionally.

Another drama unfolds when our feelings cloud our judgment. Fear can prevent disclosing our real emotions to our partner and even to ourselves. We can go through the motions with no spiritual connection, intimacy, or passion. You may be confused as to what to do, so ask yourself, "What am I pretending not to know about this relationship?" Perhaps up to now your only choice was to numb yourself and become a settler for the same and the shame.

As you begin your personal transformation, invite your significant other to join with you, do not deliver controlling ultimatums. Inspire by example, don't dictate your agenda; breathe new life into it.

CHANGE YOU AND THEY WILL FOLLOW. Invite your lover to read this book and share the journey of self-discovery. You can cross the finish line alone, but is that really how you want your story to end? Our wealth and possessions can never be fully enjoyed unless we share the experience. We are hardwired for companionship. If you have decided to make attaining peace and harmony your goal, then your intimacy with others is just as important as "closing the sale" in a business transaction.

PART II - RELATIONSHIP NO. 3
WORLD-VIEW
YOUR RELATIONSHIP WITH THE WORLD

"None of us would ever wish for the evil that was done on September 11th, yet after America was attacked, it was as if our entire country looked into a mirror, and saw our better selves. We were reminded that we are citizens, with obligations to each other, to our country, and to history. We began to think less of the goods we can accumulate, and more about the good we can do."

- George W. Bush

Is your life devoted to OBTAINING or ATTAINING? As you consider your response to this question, I want you to imagine two very long telephone poles. One pole is the OBTAINING path and the other the ATTAINING course. Your life is a climb upward, reaching for one or the other—or could it be both?

OBTAINING is the pursuit of possessions and the energy it takes to acquire them. Few of us consciously set out to OBTAIN as a goal in life. Nevertheless, the pursuit of material things can begin to take over.

The real goal should be to acquire a comfortable lifestyle with all the amenities as a PORTION of your life. Perhaps you want a beautiful, efficient, state of the art home on the coast, or in a wooded knoll. You may want a luxury car, an advanced home entertainment and electronics system, a boat, plane or a month long vacation in the South of France. OBTAINING can be a noble pursuit and you should reach for the things that your success can buy without guilt—you deserve it. The universe is abundant, our lives a reflection of it.

Then there is the elusive search for ATTAINMENT, to live a MEANINGFUL life that expresses our birth purpose, in addition to material abundance. This is the more difficult quest to define because it is so personal and ethereal. We can drive our new convertible up our long driveway and into our three-car garage. But, how do we drive freedom, peace and harmony?

To ATTAIN, then, is to experience certitude and freedom to BE WHO YOU ARE. To be free of disquieting feelings and disquieting thoughts, TO HAVE TOTAL PEACE OF MIND is entirely possible if your life is guided by principles. It is the eulogy that you write for yourself. What would you like people to say about you? What legacy do you wish to leave? OBTAINING is ME directed. ATTAINING is purpose and other-directed, and it involves, what I call, the "greater you." If we are to lead lives of complete fulfillment, we need a healthy dose of both.

Obtaining and buying possessions isn't a distraction unless it is the way that you mask perceived flaws or fill empty spiritual spaces. Sometimes we cover the holes over by identifying who we are by what we have. If you have achieved a healthy balance between OBTAINING and ATTAINING, then skip this chapter. However, if you are asking yourself, "What is the shape of my soul undressed?" or if there is any tension devoted to "stuff," or if you find yourself falling prey to the gizmos and the more than 3,000 marketing messages we are bombarded with daily, which are effectively undermining your attempts to retreat into a simpler life, often with the products aimed at helping you acquire that life—by all means read on.

Americans gorge themselves on "things" that they hope will counteract the onslaught of everything from anxiety to guilt to nostalgia. Things may not make us better, but they can make us feel better, safer and/or more connected to our past than our now and our futures—but only temporarily.

That new SUV we think speaks volumes about us as we roll around town, that expensive new suit we think projects the ambition we have yet to articulate, that soft calfskin briefcase that we subconsciously think will be a VIP pass to the future, are all just things. Likewise, the retro hammock in the front yard that cost $400, which just might be a key to our past, and, therefore, a comfort, is just a possession.

Things can symbolize dreams, new starts, and second chances. There is nothing wrong with that. However, far too often, possessions and the pursuit of them blind us. While in the chasing mode, we fail to set real goals and dream infinite dreams. In other words, sometimes in the midst of all our "hunting and gathering" many of us lose track of just what we are really seeking.

I was sitting near a woman at a party once and found myself eavesdropping on her conversation with another woman. I was compelled to listen after I heard one woman say to the other, "I love my lifestyle, but I hate my life." Wow, I thought, what a sad commentary. She was stunning in her Armani dress, slim and healthy looking, and was dripping with expensive jewelry yet, no matter what she was trying to project through her "tangibles," it was utter despair that I was hearing. We can have an almost overwhelming and pervasive sense of dissatisfaction, despite our material comforts. You can begin to sense the problem when you find yourself not seeing what you have, because you cannot keep your eyes off the horizon, because you are continually scanning for more.

OBTAINING, or materialism, can be habit-forming and as it becomes a habit, it encroaches on more important values. When objects become answers, they stifle your growth. Focusing on the next purchase wastes energy that can be used to develop a real plan, a life plan, a real sense of where you're going and who you are.

If you take the word "energy" lightly and feel that you have plenty of it to OBTAIN, then listen to the words of my 54-year-old friend:

"I love what I am doing with my life. I know who I am and why I am here. I look forward to every day with zest and to my work with complete fulfillment. Every once in a while though, I pause and think about the old saying, 'Gee, if I'd known I was going to live this long, I would've taken better care of myself,' because the only thing that can stop me from continuing a fulfilling life is the lack of energy, and my overall health. I thank God I am healthy and I have that energy. I now realize that there are only so many hours in my day, so much energy available to me to fuel my endeavors. Without my physical and mental energy, I am lost. I can not afford to waste any of it on meaningless activities or frivolous thinking."

So I ask you, what do you want to OBTAIN and what would you like to ATTAIN? What lifestyle do you see? What amenities do you require to create a comfortable life? What freedom do you ache for? What do you wish to be more harmonious? What would it be like to have no conflict with the people in your life? Imagine what it will be like to weave a thread of continuity between your thoughts, your actions and results. Do you long for peace, serenity and tranquility? All of this is possible!

You have a choice to make. Do you burn to obtain? If this is your choice then let's agree to give you the permission to acquire the things you want right now. This book is your personal tool kit. Build what you desire and OBTAIN what you want. When you get the need met and you are enjoying that lifestyle, you may experience an urge, or internal restlessness that asks, "Now what?" To scratch this much deeper itch, you have two options. The first is to reset your goals to include peace, harmony and freedom, and aim for that in every aspect of your life. You have what it takes – you will find your way. The second option is to *invest* your time and resources in mentoring others on their path.

There is another strategy that will work in your life, as well—a metaphor. Remember the two telephone poles? What if we built a series of rungs between them and made a giant ladder? The advantage, now, is that your climb is steady, stable and balanced. So, as you OBTAIN you are also ATTAINING at the same time. It is really a simple adjustment in your head. Instead of an either/or choice, you can choose BOTH. You can have your cake and you can eat it.

> *"Always act as if you were seen."*
>
> -Baltasar Gracian

The rungs between the ATTAINING and OBTAINING poles are made from your principles. This material is of high quality and tensile strength. These principles include honesty, trustworthiness, integrity, faithfulness, loyalty, respect, and doing the right thing. WITH EACH THING OR QUALITY THAT YOU REACH FOR, LET YOUR PRINCIPLES LEAD YOUR CLIMB. If you are reaching for a possession, fine and well, just make sure you reach with your principles. If you are reaching for peace of mind, the only way to ATTAIN that is through the greater you, your integrity.

Trust me, you are a principled person, or else you would have tossed this book by now. Build you and IT (your dream) will come.

YOUR RELATIONSHIP WITH MONEY

"Money ranks with love as man's greatest joy. And it ranks with death as his greatest source of anxiety."

-John Kenneth Galbraith

You must be awake for this section. If you are sleepy, go take a short nap before you go on. Perhaps it's time for ten nude jumping jacks. Don't gloss over this subject with an "I know all I need to know" attitude.

Money is a powerful tool. Self-made millionaires have developed both an ATTITUDE and an APTITUDE towards money and possessions.

Developing your money aptitude is a simple matter of gathering good sources of information and applying the knowledge. Viewing money as a TOOL (and that is truly all it is) takes all the mystery out of it and releases you to acquire the wealth you crave. The real power of creating wealth lies in your willingness to be fully conscious of your money ATTITUDES at all times. But beware, because as soon as you choose to examine yourself in this emotionally charged arena, you will likely find this axiom accurate: The truth shall set you free, but it may make you miserable at first.

We will begin to unravel this convoluted mass of feelings by asking a series of questions. Take as much time as you need to consider your responses. All of your hard work is about to payoff.

WHAT IS YOUR RELATIONSHIP WITH MONEY? Have you had a lover's quarrel? Do you feel separated? Would you be better off not dealing with all the hassle involved in a relationship with money? MONEY IS A RELATIONSHIP! Money is not the root of all evil. Your existence is tied to money, only in terms of your production and stewardship of this powerful RESOURCE. If you're not taking care of it, someone or something will relieve you of the burden. There was a time in my life that my misery sought the company of others. One day I overheard a fellow whiner boldly exclaim, "I do not have a spending problem; it's more of a funding challenge." Of course, he was being politically correct and deceptive with his words.

Do you feel capable of making good decisions with your money? Will more money change you? Will changing you attract more money? In your past, how have you looked upon people who had more money than you or your family? What did you think of them when you were growing up? Were you envious? Did you think them shallow, self centered evildoers? Did you think that, in some way, they were better than you? Did you think that, in some way, you were better than they were? Did they act arrogant with a "better than thou" attitude? Have your feelings changed? What is your current view?

What did you hear your dad say about money? How did he feel about money? What did you hear your mom say about money? What did you see her do with money? How did she feel about money?

If you had other authorities influencing you like an uncle or grandmother ask those same questions. How much of your present attitudes towards wealth are adopted or adapted from the past? What do you feel right now?

Money can certainly buy some happiness. It can buy you freedom to pursue happiness. It can provide a luxurious existence, epicurean experiences and pampering. Pleasures are for sale and limited only by your imagination.

Many of us have experienced a lack of money, either living paycheck to paycheck, or without enough coming in to cover what was going out. We have felt the shame and pain of saying no to our want, or our spouses and children's wants, because of scarcity. The stress of not being able to provide the basic needs and the crush of not being able to acquire our wants can leave us feeling defeated. The "wants" pull so hard that they become necessities for living the good life. We give them value because of the perception of joy and peace they offer us.

"The life of moneymaking is one of undertaking under compulsion, and wealth is not the good we are seeking, for it is merely useful for the sake of something else."

-Aristotle

Wealth is a noble part of life's pursuit, but it should be a BY-PRODUCT of living a value-able lifestyle, not your PURPOSE. The accumulated products can then be used as resources, funding our life in style. Money provides opportunities, YOU CAN EVEN BUY TIME. Having more time to pursue your interests and hobbies gives meaning to money. Having time and money with no plan is like living in

135

paradise with no one to share the experience. Therefore, to pursue wealth as a stand alone goal is not living the good life.

Wealth can buy you time to experience a geological wonder. We can know what it feels like to stand at the bottom of the Grand Canyon or to climb Mt. Rainier. We could take our studies on the road and explore an ancient archeological site or immerse ourselves in the sights, sounds and cuisine of a culture different from our own. We can, with enough money, provision our journey with books, teachers, mentors, and laptops, along with transportation there and back. We can, with enough money, even buy time. As an example, a friend of mine was going to visit in my home for a weekend. He is a writer who lives about 900 miles away. I remember him thinking aloud as we were planning the weekend, should he fly up, or should he enjoy the coastal and mountain views from his new car?

The fact that he could make that choice meant that he had the luxury of time. In other words, he was "rich" enough to take the extra two days to drive, rather than fly. He wasn't bound by some deadline caused by the need to work for those two days. He was literally "buying time." Time gives value to money more than possessions do. Put another way, if you were suddenly told you had only six months to live, but you could buy another year for whatever you had left in savings, would you do it?

Do you deserve more money? How much more? Most of us could use more money than we have. With respect to most of you who work for someone else, do you feel that you could ask or demand more money from your employer? Are you entitled to share more of the profits? How easy would it be to replace your contribution to the company's assets?

How much training would it take to train a replacement? I am not asking about your worth as a human being, that is, of course, invaluable. And I am not asking about such things as passion or loyalty. I am asking you to evaluate your skill set and your bartering position. What is unique about your abilities? If you can honestly answer that it would take a lot of training and time to replace you, then you have earned the privilege to re-negotiate your worth. You can take your talents and look for another opportunity to use them. Your knowledge and experience are a part of who you are. No one can take that away. Even if the position that is available has a different job description than your present position, your talents could fit into that vision.

If after considering these questions, your answers leave you feeling a bit insecure and that a replacement is only days away, you must make some important decisions. You may be encouraged or inspired to gather more training and expand your business abilities through community colleges, technical schools or apprenticeship programs. Your present company may have programs and incentives available. Most forward thinking companies consider their greatest asset to be their human resources.

If you decide to go back to school, you may find that you can only fit one course into your work-home-school interface at a time. Go for it. Prime the pump. Trust that focused effort will pay off. You may find that your schedule opens as providence moves in to co-create with you. Sure, it might take you twice as long as others to attain your credential. The realty is that if it takes you five years to acquire your new skill, that time would have passed anyway, quite likely, without a purpose, and you would be five years deeper into your present misery! So, take a step or two forward and begin to fulfill your dream today.

Debt

Debt is the ability to pretend, the larger the debt the bigger the pretense.

-"Frankly" speaking

WHEN YOU ARE IN DEBT, YOUR PAST MERGES WITH YOUR PRESENT AND BLOCKS YOUR FUTURE. Buying all of your toys and trips on time means THAT YOU CANNOT AFFORD IT. Stop pretending. You will only dig a deeper hole.

What about honoring the debt you owe others? How can you reconcile with them so that both of you can move on? Forgive yourself for past indiscretions and vow to live a more principled life. I give you permission to call all the debts owed you as well. I give you permission to say "no" to people who beg or demand to benefit from your labor with no exchange. Must you punish yourself with guilt or obligation and feel the anguish of being used or taken for granted. Enough is enough. How often have you gone that extra mile, dollar after dollar, and still the accounting ledger leaves the other person in the red?

ARE YOUR INCOMING RESOURCES SERVICING YOU, OR SERVICING YOUR DEBT?

Owing money at some point is a fact of life for most of us. One thing, however, is certain, it is not meant to be a life style. PRODUCERS earn more money than they consume, therefore, they can eliminate debt and accumulate wealth. Producers use credit cards as conveniences, not necessities. They pay cash for goods. Producers never view their cars or toys as assets. CONSUMERS, on the other hand, consume more than they produce, spending most of what comes in buying luxuries on time. They tend to buy as a response to stress, storing goods as a protection from their own insecurities, disappointments and self-view struggles. These artificial protections are volatile. They collapse and disappear under stress. Like a home built on a fault line, it's not a question of IF, as much as WHEN.

Have you become a "servant" of your own home, spending most of your free time maintaining your shelter? Do you spend your evenings and weekends fixing and landscaping, not as a source of pleasure, but out of necessity. You probably enjoy some of these tasks and the satisfaction and pride associated with a well maintained home. But, is there a more efficient way to spend your most valuable assets, time and thought? Have you ever considered that the energy that you expend may be interfering with your ability to create? Do you use these mindless activities to anesthetize you from a stressful or boring life?

Many people have made a conscious choice to downsize their responsibilities. The reality of maintaining a lifestyle that leaves no wiggle room for exploring, convinces them to play a different game. If you really cannot afford the mortgage, sell the "big house." Stop leasing the "ego sled" if the payments cause anxiety every month. You may find a greater quality of life emerging from within as a result. If you want these material possessions in your life, you can always buy them later, when you CAN afford it. However, the next time you have the money, you may not need as many toys. This time you will likely do things differently with your money and buy ASSETS, not LIABILITIES. This is one sign of a person who has used the rungs of the ladder to climb more toward the ATTAINING side of their souls.

Remember, self-made millionaires know money. Read books and seek out responsible sources to develop your "money aptitude." If something looks too good to be true, it is. Four good books on this subject are: *Rich Dad, Poor Dad,* by Robert Kiyosaki, *The Millionaire Next Door,* by Thomas J. Stanley, Ph.D., *The Energy of Money* by Maria Nemeth, Ph.D., *The Maverick Way,* by Doug Fabian.

Downsizing is a brilliant strategy. It's a conscious appreciation of how much time and quality of living have been wasted maintaining an image or belief that is in your past. Sell the house. Dump the stress. Buy a more modest dwelling and "buy some time."

My first house was a modest structure in a neighborhood of much larger homes. The thing I realized after living there for awhile was how much more leisure time my wife and I had compared to our neighbors. To maintain their lifestyles both couples worked in most of those homes. We never saw them sit on their decks, or play on the lake. They were running the rat race, not the human race.

What would you do with an extra $1,000 – $10,000 a month? How would you spend this extra free time?

"Money, it turned out, was exactly like sex; you thought of nothing else if you didn't have it and thought of other things if you did."

-James Baldwin

THRIVAL PRINCIPLES

The quintessential satisfaction in life is found in the process of training for your PEAK PERSONAL PERFORMANCE. There are natural principles at play in the universe that apply to all of us, equally. They are the Thrival Principles. Read through the descriptions and let them percolate throughout your thoughts. Accept them as truth for now. Whenever you are challenged in your life, return to these principles and see what wisdom or comfort they can provide you.

Principle #1

Success and fulfillment are naturally occurring processes. We are designed to live extraordinary lives.

Life presents us with a package deal containing both success and failure. You have experienced both. Perhaps you are experiencing one or the other right now and it is inevitable that you will experience both in your future. The good news is that only one of these states of existence is available at any given time. You can exist as a successful human being or as a failure, but not both. You can choose to give your attention to one or the other. When we look at both our successes and failures at the same time, neither one actually exists. We are thrust into a fuzziness or non-existence where we experience depression, confusion and anxiety, all at once.

Unfortunately, most of us have been trained to focus on our mistakes and weaknesses. We somehow find a way to survive in this state of failure. Sure, we get some wins and moments of success and then we hear the voice of experience, confirming just what we thought, "This won't last." We have much more experience in the game of survival, focusing our efforts toward preventing the loss rather than promoting the gain. We attempt to eliminate the possibility for failure by maintaining the status quo and slumping in our comfort zone. This approach to life causes us to shrink in the face of confrontation and avoid any decision and action that carries with it a perceived risk. Thus, fear dominates our mind and dulls our passion. We attempt to convince ourselves that if we really wanted to succeed, we could, and we defiantly proclaim, "What the heck, I'm doing better than most." When our thoughts and feelings coalesce around prevention and comfort, we generate a negative survival-only momentum.

> *"All that a man achieves and all that he fails to achieve is the direct result of his own thoughts"*
>
> -James Allen

Conversely, focusing our attention on our wins and our strengths generates a powerful Thrival Momentum. As we gain a greater self-view, our self-esteem and self-efficacy improve our ability to respond intelligently to adversity, and we attract opportunities and the resources we need to succeed. Now, when stuff happens or life's events distract you, you will blow past the obstacles. Your personal state of success or failure is a result of your choices. Other people or events can influence it, but you, alone, maintain the momentum and direction.

You and I are a part of nature, therefore, we interact with this creative intelligence. We respond to it and nature is designed to respond to us. Your thoughts, emotions, dreams and actions affect the world around you.

A recent study asked the question: Can individual intentions affect Random Number generators? The answer is "yes" according to a paper published entitled, "Correlations of Random Binary Sequences with Pre-Stated Operator Intention: A Review of a 12-Year program," R.G. Jahn, B.J. Dunne, et al. Princeton Engineering Anomalies Research, School of Engineering and Applied Science, Princeton University, 1997.

They proposed a unique model of consciousness, "Margins of reality: the role of consciousness and physical world" John and Dunne...the role of consciousness in the physical world indeed emerges endowed with an active component. By virtue of the fundamental processes by which it exchanges information with its environment, orders that information, and interprets it, consciousness has the ability to bias probabilistic systems, and thereby to avail itself of certain margins of reality. . .we can now rigorously demonstrate on the laboratory bench, and to some extent in the corresponding models, that human intention, and will, volition, desire, by any name, deployed in self-surrendering resonance with even a simple physical system or process, can significantly affect the latter's behavior, and that the same deployment of human intention with another human consciousness can condition their mutual reality to a significant extent."

Reality happens when we look at it. What do you see, success or failure? **What will you focus on, the life you want or the life you want to avoid?**

Principle #2

"A universal intelligence is in all matter and continually gives to it all its properties and actions, thus maintaining its existence."

-R.W. Stephenson, D.C.

We are not equating a design with the Grand Architect of the universe. This Intelligence was create, therefore, it is not the Creator. I do not want you to confuse this concept with a description of God. It is for you to decide whether a Supreme Being exists. I am describing a natural order. The Thrival Principles described in this book do not represent any particular religious viewpoint, but are presented for your understanding, appreciation, and conformation.

Every particle of matter, whether a constellation, mountain or human being, responds to a message. This intelligence can be verified. We observe scientific laws as simple as gravity or as complex as quantum mechanics. When you eat a French fry, you don't think about how your body is going to turn that into new cells (perhaps fat cells) or how it will go to replace the cells that make up the cornea of your eye. Universal Intelligence does that for you.

Uni=All omniscient.
Intel=Unfolding to a pre-recorded message.

In essence, ALL OF NATURE EXHIBITS A DESIGN TO BECOME ITS UNIQUE POTENTIAL. All matter responds to a set of laws. Today we look upon the law of gravity as commonplace, yet this profound discovery has transformed the modern world. Countless other laws of nature have yet to be discovered by the quantum frontier pioneers. One thing is certain, the deeper we probe the cosmos and the world of sub-atomic particles, the greater is our conviction that, with all this apparent chaos, AN ORDER DOES EXIST. There is an apparent tying together of all matter, an intelligent force binding, blending and emerging—a connection between you and every other human being, animal or plant.

Three good books on this subject are: *The Elegant Universe,* by Brian Greene, *The Quantum Self,* by Danah Zohar and *The Holographic Universe*, by Michael Talbot.

The purpose of this universal intelligence is organization. The expanse of the universe is an overwhelming concept. When we look at the starry night, we get a glimpse of the enormity of our own galaxy and an unsettling perspective as we realize we live in one of the billions of galaxies in the universe. The principle of universal intelligence simply means that there is an organizing force. Something brings order to chaos and resists entropy. In physics, we learned of the second law of thermodynamics, which states that systems tend toward disorder. The resistance to this disorder is universal intelligence. Without it, we would cease to exist. This intelligence is, quite literally, holding us together. This special principal is so difficult to touch, to prove, and yet , everywhere we look we see order in chaos.

Systems as large as our home galaxy, the "Milky Way," and as miniscule as the quantum micro-galaxies in your thumbnail follow a directive of expansion and contraction, dis-integration and integration.

Many years ago a philosopher, mathematician and scientist by the name of Buckminster Fuller hypothesized that, indeed, all of nature and the universe are constantly expanding and contracting simultaneously. Like the universe, we are made up of like energy and are, in essence, a microcosm within.

There is, indeed, motion in all of matter and as a special part of this carousel, we are tuned to thrive, not just survive. Universal intelligence has no limits!

When the universal intelligence is expressed in our own bodies, we call it "innate intelligence." This intelligence is limited in expression because of the material our bodies are made of. We can, by our own actions, interfere with the organization. We can interfere so much that our body's resistance to entropy is negated. The result is that we begin to break down and become diseased. Our thoughts become disorganized and our connection to our purpose is severed or distorted.

THE PRACTICAL APPLICATION OF THIS POWERFUL CONCEPT IS THAT ALL WE NEED TO DO IS TO HAVE AWARENESS THAT OUR LIFE IS DESIGNED TO EXIST IN A STATE OF INCREDIBLE ORGANIZATION AND THEN TO TRUST THAT AWARENESS.

You were designed to express unimaginable potentials and to interact with the matrix of life. If you are experiencing real or perceived failure, or you want a higher level of attainment, this book will help you discover how to eliminate the things that interfere with this intelligent force.

We are part of the process designed to expand and become greater than we are. You were made to ADAPT and CREATE by CHANGING and BECOMING. All of your aspirations, dreams and hopes are potentialities waiting to be expressed into existence. In reality, all of nature is ready to assist you, as long as the rules of engagement are not violated.

Later in this book, you will learn to organize your life so that you can become more conscious of how this universal intelligence is already at work within you. You will learn to experiment and risk failure, or temporary setbacks, so that you have a shot at greatness. You will become the awakened active co-creator, moving forward each day, powerfully and willingly removing all interference and impediments within or outside of you.

It is critical for your success in life that you accept that there is something at work in your life that is beyond your imagination. As you open your eyes, your heart, and your head the evidence will be there for you. Some of you will observe the footprints in the sand walking beside you, some will feel an intuitive calm and others will deem it valid by the results they achieve.

Principle #3

There is a dynamic tension between you and your environment. "Centripetal Forces" (outside of you) press in on you and the "Centrifugal Forces" (inside of you) resist this pressure, keeping you in balance.

These Centripetal stressors can be physical, mental or spiritual. Physical examples include environmental conditions, gravity, organisms (parasites, viruses, bacteria), trauma (accidents, attacks), and poor nutrition. Our resistive ability, or Centrifugal Forces determine the outcome. If we are exposed to a blast of hot air, we sweat. If we are subjected to freezing temperatures, we shiver. Healthy people respond to invasive organisms by elevating their temperatures and other important immune system responses. Physical conditioning can reduce the effects of trauma and reduce the chances of injury. Since you become what you eat, you, therefore, choose toxicity or vitality.

Mental and emotional centripetal stressors include verbal abuse, aloneness, rejection, criticism, hatred, and domination. We have all heard the expression "sticks and stones may break my bones but words will never harm me." This simply is not so. Words linger and store in our emotional recall centers. We can never truly forget the harsh words that assail us. However, our resistive resources, or Centrifugal Forces, can protect you from becoming a victim of circumstance. The strong Self-view and impeccable people skills we spoke about already, provide us with a protective shield.

Spiritual examples of Centripetal Forces may be less tangible and difficult to describe, depending upon your beliefs. Some examples of spiritual oppositions could include events that rock our faith, fear of death and dying, and a sense of not being connected to yourself. Most of the world believes in a God and accepts that evil is the opposing force. (Incidentally, you have probably noticed that when you reverse the spelling of the word L-I-V-E you get the word E-V-I-L.)

The tension that is a result of these opposing forces provides a fertile environment for growth, IT IS THE PLACE WHERE CHANGE IS BORN. Change must occur if you are to reach your rewards. Focus your efforts on developing a strong resistive centrifugal nature as your ASSURANCE policy, and stretch and grow towards your dream.

Remember this concept because it is very important: Understanding what is keeping you from your own abundance and fulfillment will help you to set up the ideal environment within your *Bodymind* and spirit for this change, or renewal, to take place.

Key to your understanding is to accept, as I have told you, that you are already fulfilled and successful—you just don't know it yet. You are like Michelangelo's David. When asked how he created his magnificent sculpture, Michelangelo replied that he had not created it. He said that David was inside the marble all along. It was just his job to chip away all the extemporaneous pieces to reveal the miracle that was within.

That is how it is with you. Your *Bodymind* and spirit were designed to be healthy, right from day one. Peace and contentment are your nature. Now you just need to learn how you are interfering with the flow of your own abundance, your own innate intelligence. Yes, you. No one else is responsible. All you need to do to tap into your own sense of profound well being is to find out how you are sabotaging your *Bodymind's* own perfection. What are you doing to block yourself from attaining complete fulfillment? Once you know this, you can begin to "eliminate" those things and/or "add" new nurturing.

From a physical standpoint, here is one example:

Some scientists now firmly believe that we are already capable of living well into our 120th year. It is not the virulence of invasive organisms that inhabit our bodies that makes us sick, it is the resistance of their hosts. Indeed, we all carry plenty of nasty organisms around in our systems, it's one of the things that builds our immune systems. In addition, when our immune systems are as they could be, the way we were meant to be, the way we were when we started, perfect—we will no longer become ill. In other words, germs don't make us sick, we make us sick. We choose illness.

In addition, we may not get enough exercise or may not eat as we should. Perhaps we've become dependent on things like sugar, refined carbohydrates, caffeine, tobacco, alcohol, drugs or any of the other harmful substances we ingest as a society on a daily basis. Do we eat for fuel and nourishment or to comfort us and dull our sense of reality? According to the American Dietetic Association, stress is the primary predictor of diet failure. As an example, following the tragedy of "9-11" junk food sales skyrocketed, Americans consumed 12.4% more cookies and chips then they did in Sept. 2000. No one is forcing you to eat junk food or to lie on the couch. These are the choices you've made, which act as barriers to reaching complete fulfillment.

Added to our physical lives, we have already talked about the fact that, to some extent, each of us is judging ourselves according to the values imposed upon us from the outside. Our internal response to these forces (our perceptions), whether that be rebellion or compliance, also determines how much stress and dis-ease we live with.

You may recall that my search for truth has required a continuous commitment to questioning all that I have come to know as reality. Like many of you I wanted to make an impact and leave a legacy. I wanted the world to be a better place as a result of my influence. Therefore, I began to study the traditional allopathic (modern medicine) approach to health and disease. I quickly realized that the study of disease left little emphasis on health. I observed the complete failure of this approach as I watched my father deteriorate as he suffered the effects of rheumatoid arthritis. Soon his career as a brilliant, dedicated detective was over. I suffered along with him as he realized that there was no cure available. He was able to have temporary relief from the pain, but the drug side effects were very unpleasant.

Principle #4

MOMENTUM is the speed or force of motion carrying you in one direction or another. The greater the density and velocity, the more difficult it is to stop, slow or reverse directions. This is true for both THRIVAL and SURVIVAL momentum.

Momentum is driven by impulses, which propel us forward toward our potentialities or backward retreating to comfort and survival. The thrival impulses of love, cognition and trust gel to form dense fuel cells, while the survival impulses of fear and anger drain these power reserves causing us to fall back, tumbling, out of control.

The power of momentum is yours to either use or be controlled by. Some have only to think and Thrival momentum ignites and propels them forward in quantum leaps. For the rest of us, it is a commitment that takes endurance, patience, persistence and faith. You have within you the ability to embrace both the lifestyle and life that you want. As your surrogate coach, I guarantee it!

Having awareness and an understanding of Thrival momentum will make the journey less stressful, more enjoyable, and a lot faster. However, at this point in the book you may be facing a rather stark awareness of the direction you are heading and how timely it is that you have started this process now. Take heart though, awareness and willingness to change directions are more than half the battle. Congratulations, if not now, when? Let's take a closer look at what might have occurred thus far in your life.

SURVIVAL MOMENTUM ejects you so far off course that you can lose sight of your goals, have a blurred view of your values, and completely be cut off from and disconnected from your purpose (SPIRIT). The law of inertia states that bodies in motion tend to stay in motion, unless acted upon by an outside force. You start to wonder why other people progress so much faster than you and these thoughts and feelings, or negative impulses, become interference and unfortunately, add to the Survival momentum. Your focus is turned inward and fear takes control. Mediocrity lowers your expectations and you learn to accept your plight, wallowing in stagnation and the recurring erosion of your remaining self-view. Not only are you gaining momentum in the wrong direction, you begin to attract a series of negative events and now, the "BAD LUCK CLUB" has a new president.

Many factors may have contributed to this stasis and SURVIVAL MOMENTUM, perhaps your lack of full commitment, denial, poor people skills, and/or a sterile life, void of purpose. There are many different ways to build destructive, or survival-only momentum, but there remains only one way out of its controlling grip. You must make a 100% commitment to the Peak Performance Process.

You will need to take what will, at first, appear to be extraordinary actions, detailed toward the back of this book, in order to fully empower yourself. In addition, you must trust the process. These principles and plans are not theories for discussion and contemplation. They are practical, logical solutions to your problems developed as a result of years of direct experience with hundreds of clients.

Work it thoroughly or become a "settler" and just dream about what could have been. For some of you this is your last chance, for others it may be your only one. Make a full commitment to arrest the survival momentum and then begin the process of building THRIVAL MOMENTUM.

If we accumulate positive impulses, we generally experience a THRIVAL MOMENTUM, which catapults us over, around, and through most obstacles or setbacks that are a part of our life experience. The denser the accumulation of positive impulses, the greater our progress. We now have inertia and momentum working in our favor. Once you start the momentum, like a giant snowball rolling down a very steep hill, it will take a nearly super human force to stop or slow the process of fulfillment in your life. The things you want to OBTAIN will be within reach almost immediately, and the ATTAINMENT of peace, freedom, and harmony in your life will be a real experience.

There is always a chance that some powerful negative event will try to knock you off course and dissipate the THRIVAL MOMENTUM, the loss of a job, a death in your family, a car accident. But because you have learned new skills from these new behaviors and thoughts The Peak Performance Process will begin to build a mental stamina, physical endurance and a spiritual strength that will guide you through any and all adversities.

Unexpected things happen and they may delay your progress, but they will never stop the THRIVAL MOMENTUM you have gained. Getting back up gets easier. By connecting with the natural process, you develop resilience and habits that will serve you for a lifetime.

CHANGE

"Resisting change keeps you from being who you really are."

-*"Frankly" speaking*

"The single greatest power in the world today is the power to change."

-Karl W. Deutsch

Change is the process of becoming who you are, pure potential. As I described earlier, as you read this book, you are in the midst of an important restoration process. Change is natural, inevitable, and part of our life journey. When you become fully conscious and embrace this movement toward your authentic self, your life becomes magical, your relationships grow more intimate, and infinite possibilities abound.

Denial or resistance toward this process causes unnecessary suffering for you, your relationships, and believe it or not, to the body of humankind. You were born with a purpose to fulfill. IF YOU DON'T DELIVER, EVERYONE LOSES.

Who am I? Why am I here? These are important questions that need to be answered by everyone in their own way. Some simply say, "I was born, put on this earth to grow and learn, to stretch my heart, leave some footprints and to pause and memorize the moments as they fly by."

Finding your own answers to these questions means embracing yourself at your core. This understanding involves CHANGE and leads to even greater growth in your life. By the time you have reached this chapter, you will have completed the assessments section and reviewed many of the coaching insights that are appropriate to your own soft-spots and strengths. Through this understanding of your "authentic" self, you will ultimately be able to answer the questions, "Who am I and why am I here?" Continue to apply the personal insights that were customized for you following each assessment. You may not have the complete picture at this time, but trust me, the pieces of the puzzle are about to fall in to place for you.

If we look at the word "change" we know that it has different meanings for everyone because of the emotions attached to it. For many, it brings up fear, for others there may be less fear and more hesitation, or second-guessing, and for some it may just be a superficial way of not committing. The fear of change is a personal monster that hides under your bed or lurks in the closet.

The actual definition has many meanings that can be extrapolated and taken in different directions. It is important in defining a word that you resonate with one or more of the meanings or synonyms so that you may connect with the actual true reasons for your resistance to change.

Change is to become different—a chance to start-over, a shift to a higher gear. Change can be a SUBSTITUTION (like in a football or basketball game where you adapt to the demands of play). In terms of your program, a better example would be to SUBSTITUTE running for smoking.

When we pass from one life stage to another, we are changing. This could be as simple as the day your mother quit doing your laundry and you had to visit the local laundromat for the first time.

Positive change may occur at incremental steps. You have clarity, fresh plans, renewed thinking. You sense intimacy in your interactions with people. You begin to have more emotional agility. You are connected with your purpose in life, and you have a feeling of freedom and peace of mind. CHANGE is certainly one of the most challenging processes of life that you face day to day. The emotional juggling is gripping on one hand—the desire for more of life, more happiness and wholeness—and on the other hand, it can be accompanied by the fears and insecurities that are a real part of change. Change is a risky venture, physically, emotionally , and spiritually.

In many people, even mention of this emotionally charged word causes severe reactions. Some of us dig our claws into the carpet, some of us find anchors and ropes to secure us to the past. We tie ourselves down, literally and metaphorically. We tether ourselves to other people, places, or things so that we can withstand the movements or winds of change that are sweeping us into our future.

Some people choose a place to live like a creek side, a valley, or neighborhood that they proudly vow they will never leave. If they are truly inspired by their surroundings then they should count themselves fortunate. They are living there by choice, fully enjoying their environment and taking pride in their community, not because they fear or resist change. No, I am talking about the self-imposed cloister in which you attempt to protect yourself. Shut off, shut in, not letting the rest of the world interact and nourish you, when life becomes so controlled and predictable that you are no longer able to enjoy the newness of a fresh idea, no longer able to feel the playful adventure of living.

What do you gain by staying put? What do you really risk by leaving? What could you gain by moving? What new opportunities await you?

Ask yourself if you aren't subconsciously saying, "I have too much time and energy invested in my misery to give it all up." Some of us get stuck on things that bring us security and comfort. It can be a house, a car, or a bank account. A thing can be a belief that no longer represents your world view, yet you hold on, tied to the past, resisting the new you, listening to the "oldies" and lying about the good old days. Nostalgia is a strong pull. It comforts us. Memories are an important part of our *Bodymind*. Enjoy the memories that a song may elicit, feel for a virtual moment, what it was like to live through that one truly free summer.

Problems are created when you feed all of your energy into what WAS. You may not have enough left to enjoy the present or engage the future. Try listening to a completely different style of music each day. Give it time. You may decide that it isn't for you, at least you've made an important effort. You don't have to like it, but at least *expose* yourself to it. You might have a hairstyle that you cling to or clothing that was fashionable but now tells everybody that you have pulled off the road and are choosing to sit here where it is shady, but not "cool."

So many of us are paralyzed by change. The fear can be gripping. The irony is, the more you resist, the more life tension you will experience. Are you trying to control life?

Or are you trying to INFLUENCE it? There is a big difference. On the surface, some of us embrace change a little quicker than others, yet the deep behavioral patterns, the current beneath, remains resistant. Staying in your comfort zone actually prolongs your misery. Most fears are selfish attempts to have the world be the way we want it to be. This "black hole" sucks all life, light, and clarity into it.

When you observe nature, do you see sameness? When you look at sand dunes, can you see the patterns caused by air in motion? When you look at the sky and watch clouds billowing and towering, changing shapes right before your eyes, you are viewing transformation. The clouds are responding to changes in unseen currents and pressures; only the evidence of change can be seen. So it is with your life. Both visible and unseen currents have sculpted you. There is a natural rhythm and tempo in your life, just as in all of nature. Like a musical composition, your life is a fusion of frenzied passages and calming verse.

"Change is the nursery of music, joy, life and eternity."

-John Bonne

SHIFT HAPPENS! You can protest aloud and shout that you do not like change, but the only people who will hear you are the ones who are stuck in the mediocrity of the pack. There will always be "room at the top," because the herd continues to feed at the trough, somewhere between greatness and futility. This is not YOUR destiny!

Did you know that your entire molecular structure will be completely replaced (changed) in seven years? That's right, the universe inside you, the forces that form your bones, heart and brain undergo continuous change and renewal. You may look in the mirror and see the same outward patterns, yet the renewal continually takes place.

Oh sure, you can struggle and attempt to delay the inevitable, and you can decline to make a decision and continue to procrastinate. HOWEVER, THERE IS A CONSEQUENCE EVERY TIME YOU DRAW BACK FROM THE NATURAL RHYTHM OF NATURE (CHANGE). THE CUMULATIVE EFFECT IS A DRAMATIC INCREASE IN STRESS AND TENSION THROUGHOUT YOUR WHOLE BODY. Like a muscle that you don't use, left alone it tends to atrophy and grow rigid, but when it's stretched and worked, it remains supple and it continues to grow.

Your innate intelligence responds to dilemmas by using any means necessary to dissipate abnormal energy in the most effective path available. This could take the form of a variety of nervous twitches such as excessive blinking of the eyes, tapping the foot, or grinding the teeth as you slumber. The more you resist change the greater the tension. You could implode a lumbar disc or create a digestive obstruction. You might vibrate your heart into a violent shaking spasm and succumb to the number one cause of death, a heart attack. (A rather chilling fact when you consider that most of the time heart attacks strike, the first symptom a victim experiences is death.)

You can't really stop change, you can only create the illusion that you're safe, protected and in control. Are you willing to continue to pay the price? How much more struggle can you bear? What is it costing you right now? Frankly speaking, it's costing you your quality of life today, and the loss of happiness tomorrow. The result? YOU WILL EXPERIENCE AN

INCREDIBLE AMOUNT OF STRESS AND ANGUISH UNTIL THE PAIN OF **NOT** DOING SOMETHING IS GREATER THAN THE PAIN OF REMAINING THE WAY YOU ARE, OR IN THE SITUATION YOU'RE IN.

As we discussed earlier, underlying resistance to change is the emotion of either fear or anger. Your immune system is weakened and, therefore, you become susceptible to viruses, rheumatic diseases, and allergies, and the common cold becomes your companion. You could experience headaches and weird symptoms that defy diagnosis and treatment. Even your mental development begins to atrophy as you cut off the learning that can occur with new experiences. You might find yourself withdrawing from the world of people who are in motion and limit your social interactions to the safety and anonymity of Internet chat rooms or the neighborhood bar where everybody knows your name, but not you. Or even worse yet, remain home on the couch, anesthetizing yourself with the television.

Overcoming "settler's inertia" gets more difficult as time passes. A body at rest tends to stay put, unless a massive force is delivered from the outside. You do not have to wait for a crisis to shift you. There is a real dollars and sense cost to resisting change.

I had a client a few years ago that was the Chief Operating Officer of a very successful manufacturing facility. His future looked bright and he even invested much of his earnings back into his company's stock. Retirement was going to be very sweet. Unfortunately, foreign competition moved in and took the majority of the market share. The board of directors were at least kind enough to let everybody know that the plant would be closing in two years, but my client refused to look for another position. Change was not something he could deal with. He did not heed their warnings. He chose to stay and traded his white collar for a blue one. The day the plant closed, he punched his time card with no plan and no stock. He is currently working for low wages, in a position with little authority, and no respect. His was another example of the strategy of boiling a frog. The tragedy was not the money and security, it was the total loss of his human potential. You may be saying to yourself that you would not be that asleep at the wheel, yet subtle shifts are occurring everyday in your life, in all of our lives. Stay alert.

Warning! Resisting and/or failure to anticipate change will cause you to wake up one morning with no place to go. The world is far too competitive to coast and assume job security. I have heard many people say they felt as if "the world had passed them by." Guess what?

Embracing change is an awkward sensation at first. TRUST THIS NATURAL UNWINDING OF YOUR FULL POTENTIAL. The transition from where you are to where you want to be can be seamless or it can be punctuated by stress, and conflict. The choice is yours. Resistance is futile.

MIND WITH MATTER

A loaf of bread goes stale as time passes because it just sits there as it falls prey to oxidation and other destructive chemical processes. Our bodies undergo a similar oxidation. However, unlike the bread, we have minds. And because we can think, we have the potential to change how external influences affect us. For years, the sages of India, China and Japan have known that their "essential" nature was a flow of energy throughout their minds and bodies—either bioelectrical impulses (thoughts and emotions) from the brain, or biochemical impulses in their bodies (now we know these are really one, i.e., the *Bodymind*).

They learned to control that flow of energy and nurture it—essentially, they learned to use the power of their minds to change their bodies. Additionally, in so doing, they were able to overcome premature aging and disease from a deeper level within their nature. They learned to use this energy and move it about their systems to keep their bodies young and orderly. This ability in a sage or master is nothing more than AWARENESS and DIRECTION of this energy.

Similarly, martial arts masters have learned to align with their *Bodymind* to develop extraordinary abilities. They have learned, through physical conditioning, mental concentration and spiritual awakening, to focus their innate energy. Because of my own training in the traditional Korean martial art, Tang Soo Do, I am able to relax in the storm of adversity. This relaxed state balances my *Bodymind ego-system* and clears the rat brain domination. When you watch the incredible feats performed by the masters of the various disciplines, you are witnessing an important principle. IT IS NOT MIND *OVER* MATTER. IT IS MIND *WITH* MATTER.

STRETCH AND GROW

I want you to know that beginning right now you must be perfectly willing to "stretch and grow." If you do this, you will not need to let go. Let me explain. While working with my patients and clients over the past 21 years, they have taught me a valuable lesson that I want to pass on to you right now. Moving from where you are right now, to who, what, and where you want to be, is no easy task.

Growing older and wiser is not for cowards. If all I do is sling a bromide at you, such as, "let go, and let God," or "Get over it" I have wasted my time and dishonored you. You may recall the song, "Breaking up is hard to do." Well, the cruel reality is that breaking from your past habits and mindsets is even more difficult. Habits, good or bad, require little effort to maintain because the choice-reason-value sequence is no longer needed. Losing old habits is a chore because you have wired your brain to behave this way. An example is watching a former smoker reflexively reaching for a cigarette after a meal or cup of coffee. However, you can go against the grain and re-wire the program. Forming a new behavior requires constant vigilance connected to a purpose. Once a pattern of success is formed, it is reflexive.

You will need courage to overcome old habits. Here is the secret **reach with all of your passion for that dream.** Stretch, as far as you can, for as long as you can. When you stretch and grow forward, the fear and the past slowly begin to loosen their grip. You have abundant opportunities to practice this new skill and measure the results for yourself. Start with little steps and build momentum to stretch for the bigger game. The Peak Performance Process is ready to catapult you to the land of milk and honey.

Perhaps you have heard of personal growth programs and team building events that put the participants through an obstacle course. I have coached hundreds of participants at various "rope course" events and, as your coach, I would like you to imagine what participants go through. Get ready for the pamper pole. The name is appropriate because they climb a 30-ft. telephone pole, stand on the top and jump off, wearing a safety harness, of course. Sounds easy doesn't it? It isn't.

I have witnessed an assortment of fear responses ranging from uncontrollable shaking, to the "bear death grip" with arms and legs hugging and digging into the pole.

Fear is not gender specific and has nothing to do with the size and shape of your body. The majority of participants have a fear of heights and the climb straight up a swaying pole compounds this fear. Sure, it's safe because certified facilitators assure high safety standards, but it still doesn't FEEL safe. Imagine yourself there. Your fellow climbers are supposed to be a part of your physical, emotional and mental support. They shout words of encouragement and, of course, when you fall, they quickly react and hold the rope as you dangle and flail helplessly above them.

Your lizard brain can slither and the rat brain can scamper up the pole, but when they sniff danger, they cling. The LOGIC of safety is, of course, obliterated by the PERCEPTION of danger. The idea is to use your sapient brain. However, the ability to rationally approach this event is very difficult. The height and swaying motion of the pole, along with the very small 18-inch surface at the top, all add to the emotional charge. The climb itself is strenuous because the location for this event is 8,250 ft. above sea level, where the air is rationed and frantically consumed in gulps. The adrenaline is flowing, your heartbeat is felt in your head, and strangers are shouting well-meaning absurdities like, "you're almost there," when clearly, you are not.

Eventually, most make it to the top and reach the last rung. Now they must simultaneously LET GO of the final hand hold and balance themselves on one foot on the top of the pole. That's right, a LET GO *and* a forward and upward movement in the same instance. Well, guess what happens? Fear locks the brain and they become frozen, feeling it's safer to stay in the security of the past (last rung), than to move into the future. The fear of letting go is powerful. Then, out of the crowd, they hear one strong confident voice asking, "What are you going to reach and stretch for?" Eventually, the climber takes a breath, engages the sapient brain and goes for it. For a brief dynamic moment they are completely unbalanced and free to fall back or forward off the pole. Somehow most of the participants make it this far, but it is too early to celebrate. Now it's time for a drum roll as the climber "hucks their carcass" off the top of the pole and into space.

"Thinking will not overcome fear, but action will."

-W. Clement Stone

There is something truly liberating in having conquered something you have always feared. The moment we take action and replace our fears with a vision, or purpose, we grow through the experience.

The pamper pole is a metaphor for adversity, feeling fear and replacing it with a goal. The example we just illustrated has an important cycle we call, the STRETCH AND GROW CYCLE. It represents:

1. Present balance (who you are, where you are now).

2. Stretching movement creates a dynamic imbalance (growth).

3. Setting a new standard balance point (Personal Peak).

4. Repeat the process.

Along the path to attaining a profound lifestyle you will encounter real and perceived risks, however you can be confident that the Peak Performance Process presented in this text has built- in protection devices. The worse case scenario is that you will remain exactly where you are, wanting to go for it, but unwilling to STRETCH and GROW.

THE GREAT ILLUSION OF CONTROL

"Except our own thoughts, there is nothing absolutely in our power."

-Rene Descartes

Letting go of control is a difficult first step for most people, not just in the rope course event, but in life. So, how do we let go of control and begin to empower ourselves? Generally, most of us feel we must have control over some things, or people, to one degree or another. Usually, this is because we don't trust ourselves, or others, in some situation. So, TRUSTING is a vital component of growth and a start to the process toward a life of profound well being.

It is in this part of your being that you learn to trust and act without "thinking," which is precisely what top athletes do when they are at the top of their game. When we watch Michael Jordan perform seemingly ultra-human moves to the basket, he isn't "thinking" consciously which direction to turn, how high to jump or how hard to throw the ball. He trusts his training, what his body and mind know and he trusts his innate abilities, the talent he was born with. He is in the zone. Had he taken the time to review each move, be like a computer, over thinking, not trusting, he would never have been the super star that he is.

You can learn to INFLUENCE the world around you, rather than TRYING TO CONTROL IT. Knowing when and which battles to choose to fight through your influence is far better than fighting everything upstream constantly by trying to control situations and people through brute mental and/or physical efforts.

Your path to the future requires that you change the vibration of your present existence (survival) to a more successful energetic pattern (thrival). You will need a considerable amount of energy to pull this off. Incompletions will pull you off track and suck your life energy until they are dealt with. They are energy leaks. Things started and not finished keep you stuck in the past. So, the quickest way to double your personal energy is to complete any unfinished business. Make a list, immediately, of all incompleted projects. These could be work or play related, anything you have left unfinished. Take each item one at a time and finish it. Do whatever it takes, but clear your plate. You may feel overwhelmed at first, simply because you are catching up, but the mess can only be cleared by you.

I have three tips for you. First, the things that are on your mind when you go to bed at night or wake up in the morning, are priority items. Second, start with small tasks until you gain momentum. Third, starting today, do complete work and finish what you start. There is no sense getting behind again. Commit to thoroughness. For instance, if the car needs washing, wipe down the inside doors and wheel wells, while you are at it.

INVEST YOUR TIME, DON'T SPEND IT

"Misspending a man's time is a kind of self-homicide."

-George Savill, Marques of Halifax

You face one more challenge in your quest to be your best. You only have 1,440 minutes each day. How will you find the time to invest in the Peak Performance Process? What can you do? The solutions will become obvious in a moment. As human beings, we use our time in three ways: work, maintenance, and leisure. The hours required to produce your income are probably the least flexible area to change. Still, look for ways to be more efficient in that area.

The next arena of time expenditure is maintenance activities. These include sleeping, eating, grooming, housework (cooking, cleaning, shopping) and transporting you and your family. At first glance, these activities may appear inflexible. However, with cooperation, delegation and prioritization, you will find ways to free up some precious hours in a week (DO NOT cut into your 8-hour sleep requirement).

The area of greatest flexibility is your leisure time activities. No matter how busy your life has become, you consume *some* amount of time during the week pursuing the following leisure activities: talking, socializing, hobbies, sports, restaurants, resting, media (TV, movies, and reading). Oddly enough, the Greek word for leisure is "scholea" and this is where we get the word school. Remember, to have a better life, make better decisions. The choices you make here will determine how fast and far you reach. When you first begin the Peak Performance Process you will need to temporarily eliminate a few leisure activities and substitute ones that contribute to your self-development directly. You can take charge and invest your time wisely by drawing from this time and energy pool. Some examples:

1. Choose carefully who you converse with. How will the conversation add to your self-development?

2. Listen to books on CD while driving and exercising.

3. Choose movies for their thought provocative quality and artistic expression.

4. Choose sports that require you to be in top physical condition (for example, basketball and soccer, not bowling).

5. Buy a lunch box and take salads and healthy drinks and snacks to work. Eat outdoors and avoid the "working lunch." Spend this time alone or with others who are passionate about self-improvement.

6. Prioritize. Do you find yourself flitting from one incomplete task to the next throughout the day? At the end of the day, do you find that the one thing you wanted to complete is still half-finished? If you do not already have a "to do" list, start one. Put the days highest priority at the top and list the rest in order of their urgency. As your day begins, start with your top priority. Do not allow yourself to be distracted by meaningless or inconsequential tasks. Focus on one thing at a time. If you have to, take the phone off the hook and put a "do not disturb"sign on your door until your priority is complete.

Prioritize your actions. If you spend all of your time solving problems, you are not resolving the real issues. Consider SELF-FAMILY-CAREER as the priority hierarchy.

"Effective people spend their time on important activities. Ineffective people live in a world of seductive time wasters."

–Steven Covey

Realize that some people are practically professional time wasters. They can fill your hours with chitchat and drivel because *they* are bored and/or selfish. You only have 1440 minutes today. Do not waste them.

I'm sure your day is similar to most of my client's. I have them keep a record of their daily rituals in order to eliminate the "time spenders" and find time to "invest" in their preparation phase. You could do the same. Make a list of your own rituals, and then stop doing them.

THINKING OUTSIDE THE BOX

How willing are you to do what needs to be done? As an example, watching television is a prime time waster. You may be saying, "Lighten up, Dr. Frank. TV is no big deal." Watching television is a habit, more than anything. It can be soothing to some, like food. It helps to fill the perceived void that there is nothing better to do for that hour in the day. Studies do confirm that some relaxation actually occurs while watching TV. However, there is no discernible residual effect once the tube has been turned off. In other words, there are no health benefits.

170

Here are some good reasons for you to kill your TV, if only for the time that I am coaching you and you are working on the plan. This could be a few months, it could be longer.

How will watching TV contribute to your energy level? Will you increase your physical stamina by watching sports? Instead of slumping in a chair why not begin the plan by engaging the real world with all of your senses, not the virtual reality of television. And that is what TV is, a "virtual reality," which can and does add to your self-view distortions. The average American watches television for five hours a day. When you are watching television and living in your virtual reality, you are essentially in an altered state—you are self-medicating, holding the real world at bay.

When you watch a volcano erupt on television it is not reality. When you listen to the sounds of the jungle, it is not real. And when you watch the Travel Channel, you are not going anywhere.

Have you ever wondered why the television has been called, the boob tube, idiot box and chewing gum for the eyes? David Frost, the British commentator, said, "Television is an invention that permits you to be entertained in your own living room, by people you wouldn't otherwise have in your home."

Television viewing can shrink your brain. Yes, there are opportunities to learn and to gather other information, but the majority of television is not geared to that purpose. Why do you think they call it "programming?" We are given a collective opinion, or consensus, depending, in large part, upon the agenda of the broadcasting network that we are viewing.

Eventually, we become numb and we start to accept the opinions of others as always being right. (The same applies to any other general media. E.g., newspapers, radio.)

There simply is not enough unbiased data for you to make truly "informed" decisions. Television only pretends to be a dialogue. In today's highly technical world, it is even striving to become "interactive." However, make no mistake, television is nothing more than a very carefully scripted monologue. After watching enough of it, we even begin to adopt the value systems of television comedies. We watch programs like "Everybody Loves Raymond" and accept that we are to remain children all of our lives allowing in-laws to dominate our actions. In addition, social maladies often become reinforced and, therefore, we become desensitized to violence. And, if you watch enough television, you are essentially becoming "incrementally" brainwashed about the world and the people around you. (Remember the boiling frog?)

We are left with the impression that all conflicts and problems can be resolved in less than a half-hour. Even when it is "to be continued" we are assured of a resolution at our next viewing. You and I both know life does not work this way. So why feed the hard drive of your brain with insignificant information; be careful to input and place only quality intelligent data.

The bottom line is that you need to take charge of what is coming into your senses when you can. The cumulative effect of television can be just enough to stop your momentum and frustrate your progress.

PART III
THE PEAK PERFORMANCE PROCESS
PHASE ONE: PREPARATION

"Luck is preparedness meeting opportunity."

- Unknown

When you make the time to prepare and patiently wait for your opportunity, you will attract lady luck. An interesting example of this is the awarding of the gold medal for the 1,000 meter speed skating event, to the Australian, Steven Bradbury, in the 2002 Winter Olympic Games. You might recall that Bradbury was a half lap behind the other competitors, including the heavily favored, Apolo Ohno. A fortuitous (for Bradbury) collision sent the other three skaters crashing into the boards, allowing Bradbury to literally skate across the finish line and into the history books.

During a candid interview, he was asked how he felt about winning the Gold medal under such circumstances. He replied that he accepted the award because of the hard work and commitment invested over the last 10 years of his life. So, you see, ten years of preparedness resulted in his qualifying for this particular race. The unfortunate calamity for the other skaters was his "golden opportunity."

"Life is fair, just not to everyone at the exact same time."

-"Frankly" speaking

Preparation is, in one respect, time travel. You are bringing your future into the present, so that you can do something about it. Imagine writing the entire screenplay to the movie about your life. You are the writer, the producer, and the director.

Look at what you desire and do something about it now. What preliminary steps will you need to take? What experience will you need to gain? What are the qualifications to be at the zenith of your career? What special training is required? What apprenticeship programs are available? Who can help you reach these goals? Who in your life is a speed bump?

UNDERSTAND THAT THE MAJORITY OF YOUR LIFE IS EITHER INVESTED OR SPENT. Make choices that promote the life you want. Invest your time, energy and money acquiring the skills and tools you will need. Stop wasting time conserving your energy and resources. How do you know that you will ever again have the freedom to soar? The window is open, spread your wings and take flight. You will discover an unimaginable gratification and joy bringing out the very best in you. I have complete confidence that the "bigness of the person within you" will come out of hiding.

Phase One is the rehearsal for your Peak Performance. It includes disciplining your body, cultivating your mind and expressing the spiritual values of love and truth. The result of the entire process is that you will take charge of your life because of a deep sense of knowing. This knowledge will be garnered from the three different sources of learning, experiential (body), intellectual (mind), and intuitive (spirit).

Experiential learning has to do with your senses. As an example, when you play a sport or perform at work, your senses provide essential information. You receive feedback from your eyes, ears, nose, skin and, yes, even your taste buds. While playing a round of golf, your visual system is calculating the distance to the green, the inner ear helps you stay balanced throughout your swing, the special sense of touch lets you feel the club, and your ears report that you hit the ball flush. This is on-the-job training for the Peak Performance Process with respect to playing the game of golf. You can consciously store and recall much of this information for future reference. Another example is a sales presentation. Your visual system is reading the facial expressions of your prospect, recording the professional plaques and making "eye contact." Your auditory system tunes you into the fluctuations in pace and tone of speech, helping you adapt to the person's behavioral style. You reach out and, with the appropriate handshake (timing and grip pressure), you seal the deal.

Intellectual learning uses your mental abilities to build your capacity to think and acquire knowledge. Thinking is a process of using your mental faculties of memory, memory-recall, reasoning, decisiveness and creativity.

A less linear path characterizes spiritual learning. Here we have a sense of awe, reverence, and wonder. Our conscious mind becomes aware, and slowly begins to accept a different kind of knowing. We name these faculties intuition or revelation. We also have terms like synchronicity to explain the connectedness of things or events that have no demonstrable causal relationship. This is that extra something that provides another level and performance edge. Learn to listen to your inner voices and trust these innate abilities!

PEAK PERFORMANCE PROCESS
PHASE ONE: PREPARATION

PHYSICAL

I know you have heard this before, yet it warrants repeating.
"Get in the shape of your life. You can not sustain or enjoy
success if you are sick and tired all the time. You must train
your body to be ready to meet and exceed the rigorous demands
of exceptional, consistent performances. Tune your physique,
build stamina and defeat fatigue."

-"Frankly" speaking

"Fatigue doth make cowards of us all."

-William Shakespeare

Every action you take, whether it is creating software, selling real estate, teaching, painting, parenting, or studying, demands a renewable source of power.

The truth is, your body is catalyzing your efforts or diminishing your potential. What special techniques or physical attributes are necessary for your career? Do you need agility, balance, or strength to perform your duties? What image do you need to project to be the best? Will a trimmer, wholesome look add to your personal portfolio? The truth is, even if your career involves riding a desk, your body must be able to handle the effects of gravity pressing on your spine and nervous system day in and day out. If you are in front of a computer all day, your eyes, fingers, hands and forearms need to be supple and relaxed for a fluid performance. In short, no matter what you do, you are a professional, train like one.

Today is the day, not next week or when you have extra time. Don't skip this part of the process, each point is a link designed to fit together. Hire a coach to help you train. All professional players invest in a mentoring program. Practice as often as you can, as focused as you can. You are only as good as your weakest link.

Exercise, diet and restoration

The Peak Performance Process begins with your physical self for two good reasons. First, you will need the fuel and the endurance to make the changes necessary to begin a life of profound well being. Your mind will have to be clear. Secondly, how you physically look and feel reflects on your self-esteem. All of us feel better, emotionally, when we enjoy what we see in the mirror.

Though your exercise plan includes weight and flexibility activities, aerobics are particularly important. When you engage in aerobic exercise, your body actually grows new blood vessels. Think about that for a moment. It's just one of the many renewals that take place on a daily basis in your body, but only if you are working at it. More blood vessels mean more blood to the brain and the rest of your organs. For this reason and others, we are going into exercise and diet first.

The mental benefits of aerobic exercise are profound:

1. It clearly improves the speed and quantity of memory recall.

2. It releases endorphins and neurotransmitters that relax us and increase our cortical alertness. Personally, many of

the ideas that come into my consciousness occur when I am running. I also find this is a great time to practice conversations with important people.

3. Aerobic exercise increases nerve growth agents which become available to the brain the and the rest of your nervous system.

4. Consistent aerobic activity builds optimism and you are less likely to become depressed.

5. It can result in an increase in capillaries around the neurons in the brain causing more blood and oxygen to reach the brain.

There are also a host of physiological benefits attributed directly to aerobic exercise. The focus of this program is to increase your mental concentration, decrease your stress, increase your energy level and build stamina. Therefore, while other people take power naps that last all day, you are shifting into higher and higher gears, tapping deep into your personal power grid.

1. Exercise: Aerobic, strength training, and rhythm activities.

2. Diet: Clean fuel only.

3. Restoration: Sleep, short naps, meditation.

It is important to first measure your fitness levels otherwise, it will be difficult to assess your progress or lack thereof. Body weight is only one measurement, and not the best one at that (muscle weighs more than fat).

Begin by measuring the percentage of your body fat. This can be done at a fitness club by either a body submersion (in water) test or by the use of calipers. Measure your flexibility and strength as well. Conduct these measurements at two week intervals. Seeing progress is a great stimulant for further progress. (Note: Caliper measurements are not always accurate. They depend a great deal on the proficiency and knowledge of the person doing the measuring.)

EXERCISE

As we've already stated, aerobic exercise is the best. Certainly stretching and working with free weights is an important part of your regimen, but aerobic exercise is going to give you the biggest energy boost and will stimulate your brain cells the most.

The term aerobic literally means "with air." Therefore, your breathing must be challenged and labored to qualify as aerobic. To benefit from these activities you must reach and maintain your heart rate at between 60% and 90% (target zone) of your maximum heart rate for at least twenty minutes, until you have a solid aerobic base, then increase to forty-five minutes. This requires a warm-up period before and a cool down period at the end of each of your sessions (e.g., 10-minute warm-up, 20-minute activity, 10-minute cool down equals a total of 30-minutes). One way to calculate our maximum heart rate is to apply the following formula:

220 minus your age = maximum heart rate. The best way to determine your heart rate is to purchase a heart rate monitor and follow the instructions to determine your maximum and minimum routines.

Most experts agree that your workouts alternate between a HARD day (80%-90% of your maximum heart rate), followed by an EASY day (60%-75%). Purchase good clothing, shoes and equipment. These investments will prevent injury and you will look and feel better immediately.

Frequency: At least 4-5 days per week. You can choose any exercise that qualifies as aerobic and mix your routines up (e.g., two days of running, two days cycling and one aerobic dance class).

Remember, stretching is a part of the aerobic cool down period and should not be neglected.

Strength Training can be added if you have the time.

Before you begin any diet or exercise program you should consult with your physician. He can also help monitor your progress along the way.

DIET

To fully explore the subject of diet and nutrition you would have to spend years of devoted study. We simply don't have the time right now, so I ask you to trust what you are about to read. I propose that we take a more practical approach and implement a way of eating that provides you with the energy and physical stamina that you will need to construct your dream.

Warning! You are what you eat. Don't waste your vital energy digesting bad fuel. Your attitude and beliefs about eating probably need to change or at least improve. So, let's begin by taking a look at how our illogical and unnatural relationship with food has resulted in rising obesity levels in adults and children alike, as well as being the primary cause of most preventable disease processes.

The harsh reality is that most degenerative and gastro-intestinal disorders occur over time as a consequence of the hand-to-mouth choices you make. Perhaps you are one of those who has gained a few pounds that you don't need. The principles we will describe here can get you started on a healthy path to building the shape you want. This is one more area that demands your full commitment, effort and willingness to change. I have seen hundreds of clients choke (literally) at this point. Do not stop now!

Diet means A WAY OF EATING, it does NOT MEAN DEPRIVATION. We eat for many reasons, one of which is fuel. Meals and food are important social interactions that connect us via dialogue and sharing. It is a good idea to try to have a family meal whenever possible. Observe holidays by breaking bread and sharing our bounty with friends and family. Celebrate milestones and victories with a good meal. The bottom line is that eating is a pleasurable experience, but at times, it is used to saturate our pleasure centers, to dull or obliterate the pains of reality. So, let's get back to basics and take a logical look at the substances we shovel into our faces.

Here are a few important concepts that can readily apply to making changes in your life starting today.

Proteins make up the primary substances for organs, muscles, bones, skin, teeth, hair, etc. They are made of building blocks called amino acids, of which there are two types, essential and non-essential. Essential amino acids must be acquired through your diet, as your body can not synthesize them. Great sources are nuts, seeds, lentils, vegetables, grains, legumes, and, of course, dairy, eggs and the "flesh foods." The point is to choose wisely from the enormous variety that nature offers. You can get all of the essential amino acids and never use animal sources, if you choose.

Carbohydrates are THE PRINCIPLE SOURCES OF ENERGY FOR ALL BODY FUNCTIONS.. However, there are dramatically different consequences depending upon which type of carbohydrate you choose to ingest. Simple carbohydrates include sucrose, maltose, dextrose, and lactose, and are contained in most fast foods and junk snacks. This type of carbohydrate is absorbed rapidly into the blood stream, giving us that glazed doughnut buzz. The problem is IT DOES NOT SUSTAIN OUR ENERGY, which compels us to consume (need) even more calories.

Complex carbohydrates (starches), such as natural whole grains, fruits, vegetables and seeds, are absorbed more gradually and provide a steady sustained power source. A way to remember this is: simple=survival, complex=thrival.

Essential fatty acids are important building blocks for your cell structure and maintenance. They are vital to your immune system and hormone production. Saturated fats are found in animal products like pork, beef, dairy, and eggs. An increased consumption of these types of foods ultimately places you in the high-risk category for heart disease and diseases of fatty degeneration. These preventable conditions, such as obesity, breast cancer, auto-immune and inflammatory diseases, are a consequence of the deposition of these fats within the cells, arteries and organs.

Polyunsaturated fats are the good guys, called the omega 6's. They are found in green leafy vegetables, seeds, nuts, grains and oils including sunflower, sesame and soybean. Another good source of fat is the omega 3's found in seafood.

Coaching Insights On Food

1. CHEW your food. The reason most people don't digest their food well is that when the food gets to the stomach it is essentially still whole. The saliva is meant to START the process of digestion and if this does not occur, the stomach is confused when this big bolus of food arrives without any differentiation between carbohydrates and protein.

2. Are you one of those people who stands at a counter stuffing food in your mouth like cattle at a trough? Take TIME to eat, even though you are busy and much of your life is spent on the run. Take time out to enjoy a meal. You can get take-out and go to a park, be creative. Many people do a decent job during the day with their meals but then the diet killers attack us between 8:00 and 10:00 at night. It is important for assimilation that you do not eat past 8:00 P.M.

3. Choose variety. Did you know that the average person only eats about 70 different foods, yet we live in a land that produces an abundant quantity and variety—well over 2000. I was raised on meat and potatoes because that is what my dad preferred and what his dad ate. I think that the first real salad that I consumed was at the age of 21. The point is, learned tastes can be unlearned when we apply logic and reasoning. If it is true that we are what we eat and digest, then you

can choose to be powerful and innovative, or weak and boring. Growth is a result of change, not routine.

4. Choose LIVE to thrive. When choosing foods, eat as many living entities as you can find. I don't mean for you to eat a hamburger on the hoof. FRESH fruits, vegetables, sprouts, yogurt, all are living life forms, ready to add their life force to yours. You must add whole foods to your way of eating. You can no longer eat a child's junk food diet and have the stamina, physically and mentally, to rocket your way to the top. Choose foods that are NOT PROCESSED and have at least some vibration and life to them. Why put poor quality gas in a pace car? Whole food burns clean with very little accumulated waste. It makes little sense to continue eating foods that are slowly building sludge (THE FAT CONTAINED IN ONE FRENCH FRY TAKES SIX WEEKS TO EXIT YOUR LIVER AND NINE WEEKS TO BE ELIMINATED FROM YOUR HEART!)

5. H_2O - Probably the most neglected part of a wholesome diet. Our bodies are 98% water. Many people suffer the subtle effects of dehydration, such as tiredness, headaches, and skin problems and never realize the solution is so simple. Quench your thirst with water not soft drinks. Start each day with a large glass of water it will help cleanse you and power your batteries. Strive to drink at least 8-10 glasses on a normal day. When it's hot or you are in an arid environment, or in a heated or air-conditioned house, you will evaporate this vital life fluid more readily, so increase your consumption accordingly. Remember that alcohol and caffeinated products draw water out of you, so you will need to compensate. As odd as this

sounds, monitor the color of your urine because a healthy person will excrete a clear to straw hue. If it is dark yellow, drink until you clear your pipes. Too much water will never hurt you.

6. You have built up a lifetime of toxic residue, even if you have been vigilant in your choice of foods. Fasting one day a week gives your digestive tract a break and increases elimination of the sludge that robs you of the energy you need to sustain your journey. Saunas, massage and other spa activities are fun ways to relax and detoxify. Also, the reason for not eating after 8:00 P.M. is that your body will be going into a "fasting" state when you retire. The longer you can fast, the better. When you awaken and eat break-FAST, you are literally BREAKING THAT FAST. So, if you have had a late dinner, try to extend the period of time in the morning before eating, to compensate. Under promise and over deliver. Don't overextend as you begin this process. It is far better to start with incremental change and as you build momentum, you can then perform massive feats. For instance, if you have a goal of running 5 miles a day and you have never jogged, start with walking, progress to slogging, shift to jogging, and then run.

RESTORATION

Most people suffer more or less from sleep depravation. Recent studies conclude that we need seven to nine hours of uninterrupted sleep and that performance drops off dramatically, depending upon how deprived we are. So the bottom line is, get rest and, if possible do what you did in kindergarten, take a 10-minute nap each day.

PEAK PERFORMANCE PROCESS
PHASE ONE: PREPARATION

MENTAL

"As a man thinks so he is. As he continues to think so he remains."

-James Allen

The power of the mind has fascinated and frustrated humankind throughout history. We all understand the wisdom of positive thinking, yet collisions with the real world don't always leave us in a positive mood. Current research in the *Bodymind* interaction confirms that we are only as healthy and fulfilled as the quality of our thoughts. Fascinating studies are suggesting that our thoughts are a form of energy that interacts and changes matter.

The purpose of this book is not to prove such theories. I can assure you that hundreds of case studies and personal experiences substantiate the impact that our mind has on our destiny. We affect ourselves, those in our life, and the substrate of matter.

The purpose for mental preparedness is obvious. If we can't think, we are unable to understand our circumstances or make course corrections. If we can't think, how can we imagine or dream? If we are mud headed, how on earth can we make correct choices? Your mental preparation can never end. Study as if your livelihood depended upon it, because it does. Learn all that you can about the sport or career in which you intend to excel. Knowledge gives you the power to act with certainty and mindful focus. When you place your full attention in any area of life, the rewards are dramatic. Rediscover for yourself the power of concentration and the ability to focus your mental intentions. Just as a reminder, we are preparing for the best performance possible in all that we do. Every day is a potential Peak Performance !

If your mind is not trained to focus, you will perform poorly. Let me give you an example. People who play golf love to hate it. The above average player practices the physical skills adequately, yet his or her game is rarely consistent. What do you think causes these poor performances? You're right, the game is mentally taxing. For one thing, the pace is much slower than work or most other sports—the average time that a golfer is actually hitting the ball in a four hour period is only three minutes. What do you suppose happens in between shots? Right again. The "rat brain" has too much time to THINK. Players who have developed mental powers of concentration and the ability to stop the emotional kidnapping win at life and sport. Like the better golfer, they learn to let go of control and to trust their abilities, regardless of how much time they have between shots.

You may be saying, "I wasn't the best student in school." Well, there is a huge difference between who you were then, and who you are now. It is so much easier to enroll in classes or teach yourself when you have a vision and a passion for it. All of my clients are absolutely astonished by their dormant mental talents once we reawaken them.

It is this simple, "Where your interest lies, your mind thrives." When your mind is absorbed, it doesn't wander or become so easily distracted by the speed bumps in life. The learning technologies and interactive formats of our new age make mental training a lot more efficient, effective and fun.

Curiosity may have killed the cat, but it awakens your innate power to create and reason. The sleeping dragon of wisdom, once aroused, is not easily slain. (If you still haven't figured out what your passion is, review your scores on the Values Assessments.)

What graduate level or technical courses do you need? What direction is your industry moving? What will you need to know to be a consummate competitor? You must feed your head. GROWING A BRAIN IS A NATURAL DEVELOPMENT OF AN ALREADY EXISTING POTENTIAL. Download innovative information and research from the Internet because your studies should integrate these new concepts with the traditional teachings in your area of interest.

This is the part of the preparation phase where your primary focus is your intellectual development. However, as your database expands, you will be integrating the experiential and spiritual knowledge. There are three levels or stages of learning.

First, there is the simple knowledge gained through the observation of things. As an example, if you look outside you might conclude, "I know the sun will rise and set sometime tomorrow."

Secondly, comprehension is to grasp something mentally and perceive its relationships to certain other facts or ideas. The earth's axis of rotation determines sunrise and sunset as it takes 24-hours to complete a rotation.

The third level of learning is called understanding. This is to be fully aware not only of the meaning or nature of something, but also of its implication. To continue the same example– "I know that the rotation of the earth not only effects the cycle of day and night but it also has a dramatic affect on weather, crops and human productivity."

When you develop all three levels of learning, you will have earned wisdom. Keep asking the right questions, in the right form and your answers will appear. Level three knowledge, wherein you understand how things fit together, also helps to defeat worry and other stages of anxiety.

As a precaution, safeguard your work by pondering the worse case scenarios. I do not want you to plan for failure, I want you to prepare for the outside forces that can knock you off course. You can ill afford to be caught in any situation without a back-up plan. Anticipate the best-case scenarios. When your plan is working even better than you imagined, you will need to be agile enough to leap ahead to the next part of your training. Life is sometimes like a computer game, when you win you are automatically kicked up to the next level of difficulty. Maybe you were not expecting that promotion to come through so soon. Now that you find yourself in the next game, you will need to sharpen your present skills and acquire new ones that fit management and leadership.

Learning is like eating a fine meal, acquire the knowledge, ingest it, ruminate over it, digest it and assimilate it into your being. Then release anything you cannot use. Stay alert, fully conscious, while experiencing the confirmation of the things that you already know to be true and the pliability to accept radical new information.

BRAIN HYGIENE: MENTAL FLOSSING

Did you know that you can continue to learn at any age? It is true that we are born with a certain number of neurons (nerve cells), and we do lose these as we go through life. However, neuroscience confirms that we have a constant capacity to grow new neural connections. It is the interconnectedness of these neurons that give us our mental powers.

Intellectual learning, experiential understanding, and spiritual contemplation are all enhanced and expressed from these neural networks. I've heard people remark, "That dog won't hunt," meaning they have given up because they can't even see the possibilities. The "I'm too old to learn" excuse just isn't true. A mind is a terrible thing to waste. We are all born with an incredible capacity for intelligence. In fact, as I have stated throughout this book, we are born with everything we need.

The universe is filled with knowledge ready to be absorbed and put to use. There are libraries, the Internet, consultants, books, magazines, the list is nearly endless. Become a person who is not afraid to ask questions, one who readily and eagerly seeks knowledge and help from others. Surround yourself with people who demonstrate strengths in areas different from your own.

Absorbing knowledge is essential to your becoming who you are. It is the key to reaching your goals, the immediate, as well as the infinite. It is essential to interpersonal relationships, be those social or business. Without knowledge, self-empowerment is impossible.

In addition to learning, you may need to unlearn some things in order to make room for fresh ideas. Challenge your perceptions. UNLEARN AT LEAST ONE CONCEPT TODAY. In other words, pay attention to the things that are NOT working, as well as those that are.

Trust your intuition, those "gut feelings." Some people refer to a sixth sense that helps them achieve greatness. Remember, we all have the same Thrival instincts, some people learn to tap them more easily. Trust your intuition and act on its urgent message. These innate senses need to be exercised to gain their potential power in your life.

Develop your aesthetic awareness by experiencing the arts, musical performances, theater, and galleries. Buy Michael Napoliello's book, *Nine Famous Artists Your Children Will Love,* even if you don't have any children. Travel to a different city, immerse yourself in a different culture.

Read. We read for entertainment or to be informed. Right now, it is important that you choose books that are thought provocative and informative. Provocative reading stretches you intellectually, challenges your current beliefs, poses possibilities and stimulates your imagination. You will not only think outside the box, you will be living there. Informative reading will add to your current knowledge base and assist your transition to a career change or promotion.

Thinking and understanding is a process, not an event. Your degree was a commencement exercise, a beginning, not a finish line. You must read a minimum of 20 minutes a day. Subscribe to a newspaper or two. Get the Wall Street Journal sent to your home because it is written at a higher grade level than most newspapers. Subscribe to magazines like Psychology Today, Scientific American and avoid the gossip type publications. The point is to provoke thought, not reinforce emotional patterns.

Viewing

A nun, Sister Wendy Beckett, who wrote, "Sister Wendy's Story of Painting," spent 27 years in total seclusion. Though she is no longer an isolate, she continues to practice silence and prayer seven hours a day. Most of this time is simply spent "viewing" art, usually prints and postcard reproductions she keeps in her room. Viewing actually does not accurately describe her process. She calls it, "quiet attention," or looking with awe and wonder. She says that if she looks long and hard enough at a painting—even one she doesn't like—it begins to take on a life of its own and she is able to see why it's considered a great work of art. This phenomenon has also been called the "growing eye" because it expands as it learns to participate emotionally and spiritually with the object itself. When we engage not only the naked eye but the growing eye as well, we begin to see the extraordinary within the ordinary. You don't have to spend 7 hours a day viewing but take some time each day to reflect by viewing something beautiful and allow your growing eye to see something extraordinary that you didn't see before.

Dreamscape

Dreams are those visions that create your destiny. When you dream, what do you dream about? In the beginning of this book, I asked you to describe your perfect day. Is your answer the same as it was then?

Without dreams or goals, there is no hope for the future, and without hope, there is despair and negative thinking. In many ways, your goals define you, that is why it is so important to have the strongest possible goals you can imagine. You are not the sum of your accomplishments or failures. You are not the very worst or the very best thing you have ever done. You are your dreams and your actions upon those goals. Your goals are a map for getting where you want to go. By now, through your answers to the Values Assessment, you should have a clear idea of what your passions are. Without a clear understanding of what your passion in life is, it will be nearly impossible to set meaningful goals and to dream infinite dreams.

Achieving your goals requires that you first define what it is that you want and then begin to work to get it (OBTAIN-ATTAIN). Eventually, as you begin to implement these daily action items we are discussing and your own customized plan (based upon your responses to the Assessments), you will realize that these dreams or goals are your only competition in life. Once you have set your goals down, there will be no further reason to "want" what other people have. You will only want to reach your own goals.

Much has been written about the power of imagination. The bigger the vision, the greater the success. Your imagination is limited only by your self-view. This is precisely why we are placing so much emphasis throughout this book on improving the relationship you have with yourself. The power to imagine, to form mental images outside of our senses, and to grasp concepts helps us transcend difficulties and create vast resources. Take the time to daydream.

Understand that having a creative imagination is not only reserved for artists, poets and philosophers. Define what you want, as we discussed in the very beginning of this book. Find out what your passion is and make that your supreme goal. Your imagination gives you a picture of your goal from which to begin work. We always act and perform in accordance with what we IMAGINE to be true. Realize that we have been engineered as a goal-seeking species. When we have no goals, no dreams or interests, we are apt to go around in circles like a boat without a rudder, feeling bored, aimless and lost, without a purpose. Your goals or dreams are your roadmap for getting to where you want to go.

Achieving your goals is a two-part proposition. First, you must define what it is that you want (passions) and then you must work toward achieving it.

Many people fail, even after they understand what their goals are, by "giving in" to that little voice in the back of their minds that immediately gives them a dozen reasons why they will not succeed. It is important to believe that all your goals are possible to achieve. You have the power to "imagine," therefore, you have the power to make that "imagined" thing a reality. What the mind can conceive the body and spirit can achieve.

Your brain and nervous system constitute an extraordinary "goal-striving mechanism." You have a built-in automatic guidance system which can work wonders for you as a success mechanism. You have been engineered as a part of goal-seeking species. Consider this example of the extraordinary powers of the mind: A subject under hypnosis, when told he is at the North Pole, will begin to shiver and appear to be cold. His body will act in accordance with his perceptions and he will react just as if he were cold. In experiments, other hypnotic subjects who were asked to imagine that one of their hands was submerged in ice water, demonstrated thermometer readings showing that the skin temperature in that hand did drop significantly. Tell a hypnotized subject that his finger is on fire and not only will he grimace, but his cardiovascular and lymphatic systems will react accordingly. IN SHORT YOUR NERVOUS SYSTEM CANNOT TELL THE DIFFERENCE BETWEEN A REAL OR AN IMAGINED THING. Your system reacts appropriately to what you think or imagine to be true. Knowing this, can you now see that you are your dreams?

Your first step is to set a goal or dream. The second is to imagine it to be true from the moment you tell yourself what it is. This is called mental imaging. Form a picture in your imagination of the self you want to be and then see yourself in this new role. This is vital to becoming who you truly are. Make these pictures as vivid and detailed as you possibly can. You want your mental pictures or dreams to approximate actual experience. Do this by paying attention to small details the sights, sounds and objects in your imagination. The details are important because, for all practical purposes, you are creating a real life experience, insofar as your nervous system is concerned. If your practice is detailed enough, it is real. As your dreams begin to come true, you will become a stronger believer in the infinite possibilities before you. You will begin to relax more, knowing you have the power to achieve anything you set your mind to. You will be empowered. Napoleon Hill, in his classic book, *Think and Grow Rich*, interviewed many of the world's wealthiest and most successful men of his time men like, J. Paul Getty, Nelson Rockefeller, Dale Carnegie. He found that along with the many similar attributes these men shared, the most important seemed to be the ability to set monumental goals, the kind of goals that were beyond the comprehension of the average person. He also found that once they set these goals, they immediately began to see themselves in the situation they desired. They never worried about how this would come about, never waited for the outcome to physically transpire; they just acted as if it were already a reality. In fact, Hill found, in many cases, these men didn't have a clue when they originally set the goal, as to how they would succeed. They just assumed they would; failure wasn't an option. Hill says, "They just TRUSTED that it would happen as they set about finding the knowledge they required to actualize their visions."

These men knew they did not need all the knowledge in the universe to achieve their goals, only an overwhelming desire and enough information to begin to act upon those desires. They were certain they would find all the information they needed, when they needed it. Like Napoleon Hill wrote, "It is imperative to see things as done, rather than as possible."

PLANNING FOR YOUR LIFE

"A life not planned is not worth examining."

-Aristotle

Planning is bringing your dreams and desires from the future, into the present, so that it can be touched, molded and worked.

The act of planning and contemplation clarifies your vision and strengthens your resolve. I want you to know this,

YOU WOULD NOT HAVE THE DREAM UNLESS YOU WERE CAPABLE OF ATTRACTING AND MANIFESTING IT. That's right, it is your dream for a reason.

Planning includes setting reachable goals, in all aspects of your life, on a timeline. Much has been written on the subject of goal setting, and because it is such a powerful tool, it warrants further discussion. The act of thinking transforms the abstract into the tangible. When we conceive ideas, we give birth to realities. When we dream and unleash our imagination, we become co-creator's, active participants who determine our own fate. Creating does not imply that we are God. We are not creating a "some-thing" from a "no-thing." Instead we are taking fragments and pixels that already exist, aligning, and focusing them. The result is a unique form that has never existed before.

History provides rich examples of creators such as the inventor of the printing press, Johann Guttenberg. He accomplished this creative movement by focusing on what he wanted and letting go of fear. He became focused on the challenge and viewed success and failure as part of the process. In a flash of insight, he combined two successful inventions, a winepress with a coin stamp, and the printing press was born. The world changed at that very moment. What if he had succumbed to the fear of being criticized and thought foolish? How long would humankind have remained uneducated? Perhaps the "information highway" would have never been built. You have the same ability within you, perhaps it's dormant, or blocked. Reach in and birth your idea, the world is waiting! Here's one model to help explain how your thoughts change the world around you. Our thoughts continually charge the "field." This "field" is what quantum theorists speculate to be the interactive substrate of the universe. When we form thoughts, our ideas affect these subatomic particles that comprise matter.

There are a host of great writers and scientists who are dedicating their lives to exploring the micro-universe and bringing their discoveries to our conscious awareness. It is important that you understand the implications of these incredible concepts. Discover for yourself how setting a goal brings that thought into being.

I would like to let you in on another secret, you are having an impact on the world. Your conscious and subconscious thoughts move matter. Do not let this power become corrupted or wasted on worry and fear, because the things you think about most, manifest. I challenge you to take responsibility for your thoughts and to eliminate the chattering monkeys that pull you back into the jungle of mediocrity. Your conscious actions bring you closer to your destiny. Stay awake, be attentive! We are unique and, therefore, we leave a distinct impression and lasting legacy for humankind to inherit. What will be said about you? How will your actions benefit the generations that follow? Do you choose to discipline your mind and develop your mental prowess? The only other choice is to accept your plight and be content as a cow, ruminating over your possibilities. Cows ruminate, they chew over and over again. Human beings swallow life whole.

Now that you have made the choice to use your brain and change the world, we will need to define a few very important concepts motivation, intention and goals. Motivation is the "fire in your belly" that ignites your passion and powers your behavior. Motivation is a movement from either inside or outside of you. It is an action or behavior in pursuit of a goal, desire or dream. When we are motivated, we are literally stretching toward what we want to have happen. There are two types of motivation, intrinsic and extrinsic. It is vital that you distinguish between these two sources of energy at work in your life and become conscious of what is attracting and pulling your energy.

Intrinsic motivation occurs when we are driven, from the inside, to take action on a plan because we want it. Extrinsic motivation occurs when we're driven, from the outside by some circumstance or person because we need it. This distinction will provide understanding and empower you with choice vs. "have-to" reactions to your life circumstances. It is my opinion that when you are moved from inside, you are balanced and connected with your *Bodymind* and spirit. When you're moved from the inside, the actions and decisions you make tap passions in your inner core. Maybe you have always wanted to be a doctor, CEO or entrepreneur. When you choose to take action on these goals and aspirations, it is pure passion, because you want it, you dream it, you become it. If, on the other hand, you are driven to pursue these careers because others expect it of you, it is by emotional need, not choice. Be cautious here, for you run the risk of living a counterfeit life, pushed here and there by feelings, duties and obligations. I want to give you permission to pursue goals and to take action that originates inside of you, and because it is what you want, not what they want. Take a moment and go back to the Values Assessment. Remember, your top two are drawing you from the inside out. Every goal you form and action you take should answer this question, "How will this satisfy my personal value system?"

An intention is a direction, aim or purpose that comes from deep within you. As we take responsibility for our lives, we know that, indeed, we are successful co-creators. Most of the circumstances, situations, relationships and material possessions that we have, we attracted to ourselves. Using intention, you will learn to manifest what you want into your life.

Intentions are potent mental lasers that guide you and obliterate obstacles in your path. A life without intention is in chaos. Imagine trying to navigate the Pacific Ocean without a GPS or other navigational aid. You must first know where you are and then have a direction or location in the future in which you want to appear. When you identify your purpose, you bring meaning and significance to what you want to create. This visceral bond between you and your goals becomes unbreakable. If you have not identified your purpose, do not worry. Continue to read this book and interact with the assessments and questions and your purpose will find you.

A goal is an object, situation or area toward which your energy is directed. An object is a possession you want to obtain, such as a car, house or money. Your goal may be to create a situation, such as finding a career or a new position with the earning potential to capture and protect the lifestyle you desire. Another situation toward which you extend energy may be in the area of romance. The process of attracting that special person who shares your mind, spirit and, of course, your body, is a great example of what I call the "quantum dating service." Many of my clients have discovered a potent aphrodisiac that is guaranteed to attract a mate, DO NOT BE NEEDY. When you reach for companionship out of lack or need, you will repel healthy relationships and become a magnet for drama. However, if the motivation is from the core, you suddenly become a powerful "dating magnet."

Something magical happens when you blend your intentions and goals. Use this natural synergy to increase your self-awareness and strengthen your certainty and self-efficacy. As an example, you may want to run five miles a day as a goal, and your intention is to be physically fit. Therefore, one compliments the other. Another goal may be to purchase a new home in a gated community and your intention is to be financially sound, so that you have the option. Blend the two and watch the distance between the present and your future diminish.

Imagine yourself sitting on a white beach at sunrise. As you look out over the gentle waves, you see a vast series of islands stretching far out over the horizon. The goals that you wish to reach are like setting foot on these lush islands. Keep in mind that this is a quest with a series of bridges and beach landings. Your quest must be planned and well provisioned or you will find yourself a castaway, living a desperate life of survival.

NOW USE ALL THE RESOURCES AND ENERGY AVAILABLE TO YOU SO THAT YOU CAN CONSTRUCT TEMPORARY BRIDGES BETWEEN WHERE YOU ARE AND WHERE YOU WANT TO BE. THESE BRIDGES CAN NOT BE PERMANENT, AS IT CAN TEMPT YOU TO HALT YOUR CONQUEST OR WORSE, GO BACK TO THE PERCEIVED SAFETY OF THE PAST.

COACHING INSIGHTS

1. You must commit fully to the process of success. When you commit there will be no chance to draw back or hesitate. If you

hear yourself saying, "A part of me wants it," stop and reload for a goal that "all of you" desires.

2. Set reachable goals. They should be out of reach but not out of sight. It is important to stretch yourself beyond the present, yet this must be balanced so that you have the self-efficacy to press on. Setting unbelievable goals will only discourage you.

3. It is important to keep a wide-angle perspective as you view all of the island goals you wish to land upon. Just as you are about to set foot on one, plot the course to the next beachhead.

4. It doesn't matter whether the goals that you reach are large or small because you will be gaining momentum. The moment you look back, you abruptly come out of the experience. While it is important to celebrate your accomplishments and mark your milestones, stay in the present and nurture the experience from there. Briefly, acknowledge how far you have come, give yourself a high five and get back in the water.

5. Before you go to sleep, invite your dream. Your subconscious will work on it while you sleep. Place a pen and paper or voice recording device on your nightstand. Your innate flashes of creativity must not be forgotten.

> *"Watch your thoughts; they become words. Watch your words; they become actions. Watch your actions; they become habits. Watch your habits; they become your character. Watch your character; it becomes your destiny."*
> -Frank Outlaw

Remember, unless it is written, it does not exist. Take pen in hand and write your future. This template will help you organize your goals in three categories: personal, professional, and community. Each of the categories are divided into three time periods to help you plan your future: short range, medium range, long range. Here are a few suggestions to get you started.

PERSONAL GOALS

AWARENESS AND DEVELOPMENT

Physical: Health (not just fitness), strength and endurance, ideal weight and body fat percentage, biological age in line with chronological age, comely appearance.

Mental: Clarity, discernment, memory, pursuit of knowledge (experiential, academic and intuitive).

Spiritual: Discover your origin and destiny by asking yourself, "Am I a human being who is having a spiritual experience, or am I a spiritual being having a human experience?" Accept synchronicity (synchronism of events that appear to be connected, but have no demonstrable causal relationship).

WEALTH AND ABUNDANCE

Wealth: Debt reduction, wealth accumulation (retirement plans, bonds, stocks, etc.).

Abundance: More cash flow and discretionary income, great home (do not equate size with quality), new car, art, furniture, toys (skis, boat, golf clubs, clothing, etc.).

PROFESSIONAL GOALS

CAREER MASTERY

Career mastery (being the best you possibly can at what you do for a living): higher education (graduate courses, further technical training), experience (doing), expertise (knowledge and experience), exploration of new career opportunities.

COMMUNITY GOALS

WE-GO vs. I-GO

Support your community, participate in a just cause, love and serve humankind.

Take as long as you need to write down the goals that are attracting you right now. Then come back to this section later to add and review. This is your life, your manual, your dream, share them only with people who will support you and hold you accountable.

PERSONAL GOALS

Short-range (3 to 6 months)

Medium-range (6 to 18 months)

Long-range (1-1/2 to 3 years)

PROFESSIONAL GOALS

Short-range (3 to 6 months)

Medium-range (6 to 18 months)

Long-range (1-1/2 to 3 years)

COMMUNITY GOALS

Short-range (3 to 6 months)

Medium-range (6 to 18 months)

Long-range (1-1/2 to 3 years)

PEAK PERFORMANCE PROCESS
PHASE ONE: PREPARATION

SPIRITUAL

Have you ever been told to avoid discussing politics and religion? So have I and yet I'm compelled to share with you a couple of insights and distinctions. Why don't we proceed by exposing another "they said" myth? Allow me to digress for just a moment. Do you get just a little annoyed when you hear the "they said" argument? Here is a terse response you can use when people say, "They won't approve of that," or "They want you to do it this way." You very politely ask, "Who specifically?" You will be amazed how this simple query locks up their hard drive. Thanks for indulging me, now I'll get back to our discussion. The topic of spirituality is separate from that of religion. A religion contains a specific fundamental set of beliefs and practices. I am not avoiding the subject. It's just that I have a profound respect for your personal beliefs. Like you, I am thankful that we live in a nation in which we are free to practice our beliefs. Most religious people that I know are deeply spiritual.

Spirituality is the awareness of the intangible and the pursuit of all the immaterial qualities of life. It acknowledges that special something that both separates us from, and at the same time, connects us to the rest of the universe. Spiritual preparation is a very private matter. The search for significance, meaning and purpose in your life is undoubtedly the "peak of ATTAINment." Spirituality can be a personal relationship between you and God. For others, it is an awareness of something beyond the five senses.

Still many people have not had the time to explore their spiritual nature. Yet, it is obvious, that all human endeavors benefit by developing and opening this window to the spiritual values of love and truth. If you have a relationship with your maker, have one of you become the "silent partner"? Perhaps you are not asking the right questions. Hook up and have a heart and soul conversation. Don't just pray, learn to listen and receive, and then accept guidance. It's all there for the asking. There are many ways to quiet the mind and allow space for that special extrasensory input. I encourage you to find the path that is right for you. It's your journey, take the time you need.

Experience a variety of paths to find the one that connects for you. Some people need the solitude of a cloister, others need the tranquility found in nature, and still others can meditate in rush hour traffic. Learn to quiet and rest your mind each day as you anticipate insightful, intuitive flashes of directions. Many people find that the light of dawn brings a flood of creative ideas and insights. Get to bed early enough so that you don't miss the show. Intuition and insight are the gateways to the Peak Performance Process.

Your spirituality is part of your makeup. Tap this resource and ATTAINment follows. The benefits are temporal as well. This study illustrates an important benefit. Research from the University of California at Berkeley found that Christians and Jews who attended regular services lived longer and were less likely to die from circulatory, digestive and respiratory disorders. It should be noted that the researchers came to the conclusion that an unshakable inner peace is the common denominator. They further concluded that if the studies had included other religions or spiritual disciplines the results would be the same.

SPIRITUAL DISCIPLINES

LOVE YOURSELF. LOVE OTHERS. The best spiritual gift you can give yourself and another is unconditional, "no-strings attached," LOVE. Do not expect a reward. Always expect to give more than you receive. Take a "this one's on me" attitude. Go out of your way to help and share with people. The good feeling you derive will be your reward.

THERE ARE NO SAVINGS ACCOUNTS FOR LOVE. Since you can't save it up, why not spend it? The great thing about love is that you can never give it all away. You can spend it freely every day, as much as you like. It's the one thing that you can be extremely extravagant about. In fact, the more you give it away, the more you get back. It's an endless loop. When I use the word love I mean several things, including forgiveness, caring, sharing, bringing out the good in others, being a good listener, helping other people, in general, what we call, the GREATER YOU-oriented things in life.

See the good in others. You cannot ATTAIN inner peace and well being unless you love. Try, today, to see something positive in every person you encounter. Why should their flaws and negatives be the first things you think about? Because they are more obvious? Then dig a little deeper. Loving others isn't just a matter of being nice. Love must be engaged in with a specific focus and intention. When we strive to up-lift others, they move closer to their own awareness and so do we. When you see the good in others, talk about it, expand upon it. The more you uplift someone, the more you uplift yourself. Make an effort every day to lift each person's spirit that you meet.

LOOK FOR WIN-WIN SITUATIONS. A win-win situation is when both sides come away feeling positive. Creating these kinds of outcomes in your interpersonal relationships will help you keep your ego in check. It also serves to remind you to keep an open mind about another person's point of view. Since you can't control other people and shouldn't attempt to, always keep an open mind. See the other person's point of view and how you can let her walk away with dignity. What will you give that person so that she can feel she has won something? Understand that this may mean altering your behavior and becoming more adaptable. A person with a BALANCED EGO-SYSTEM is always looking for a win-win. They don't need the "high" of winning all the time, they are more evolved than that. Follow the Platinum Rule, *"Do unto others as they would have you do unto them."*

We demonstrate our love for others through our *Bodymind* and we receive love through these same senses. When we experience love through our positive emotions, such as happiness and joy, there is a natural alignment of *Bodymind* and spirit. We have a Thrival resource of energy to use and share. As we talked about earlier, love can be expressed through the negative controlling emotions as well. While love can leave us feeling sad, hurt, angry and afraid, it is our choice to remain miserable and shut out the light.

DO THE RIGHT THING. I believe that, regardless of religion, culture or our own upbringing, everyone intuitively knows what the right thing to do is, in every situation. That does not mean we always take that path, but down deep inside, we know what is right and what is wrong. Strive to do the right thing in all your relationships and all situations on a daily basis and within every encounter. TRUTH is a universal spiritual value. We learn and discern through our *Bodymind*. This is a natural design and, as we have seen, emotions can cloud our perception, acceptance and sense of right and wrong. Discipline frees you to see differently. The truth is constant, persistent, and good. Let it find you, let it in. Strive to live a virtuous life. Begin by always telling the truth. Your words must agree with your thoughts. Say what you mean and mean what you say. Lies sabotage your efforts and are huge blocks to a Peak Performance.

Try this experiment, for one month do not engage in any form of gossip about anyone. Go 30 days without saying anything negative about anyone, including yourself. Once you have promised this to yourself, you may be surprised, at first, at how many times you begin to say something negative and then catch yourself. After a while, you will become aware of how many times in the past it was easy to say something negative or to gossip about someone you truly had no first hand knowledge of. Within a short period, you will find yourself either not speaking out or, even better, you will find yourself striving for a positive comment instead. In the end, you will feel much better about yourself and you will have found yourself gaining some insight about other people, insights about their good sides.

BALANCE YOUR EGO-SYSTEM. You expend the least amount of valuable energy when your choices and actions are motivated by love. When you seek power or control over other people, you are wasting a lot of valuable energy.

LET GO OF CONTROL and, if you must, replace it with INFLUENCE. However, remember, you don't have to influence everyone or every situation. You have your own goals to work on, they are your only competition in life.

One of the greatest energy stealers in the world is egocentricity, which is concern for self exclusively. Seeking approval or trying to control uses up an inordinate amount of energy, physically, mentally, and spiritually. Here is a way to build up a healthy ego, make a commitment every day that you will accept people, situations, and circumstances as they occur. It is not your job to change the moment, condition, or person. Your only focus is on being the best you can be in all that you do and to ATTAINING your goals. When you struggle against situations and moments, you are struggling against the entire universe, because the universe is as it should be.

As you begin to accept people and the world "as is" and focus on your own goals and passions, you will begin to ATTAIN peace of mind.

THE PEAK PERFORMANCE PROCESS
PHASE TWO: PERFORMANCE

Performing is the actual "DOING" part of the process. The "performance event" is your opportunity to test your abilities and experiment with new approaches. This is the place to gain crucial experiential knowledge. You learn what works for you and what does not. If your preparation is sufficient, you will not flounder. If you fail to hit the target , no worries, make the adjustments during the next practice session. The performance event is an important happening and it is connected to all of your previous efforts. Remember that it is not a make or break situation. We have been emphasizing the development of your mind. Now is the time to quiet your thinking and shift to a tranquil focusing of your mind. I know it sounds contrary to what you have come to expect, trust me, critical thinking during the performance will result in an ineffectual and strained execution.

"If you ask a centipede how he walks with a hundred legs, he stumbles."

-Chinese proverb

When you are in the performance mode, you are so caught up in the movement of the moment that you have no space left for extemporaneous thoughts. If you become distracted by fear or celebrate out of phase, your timing, rhythm and choreography will suffer. Your performance will be choppy and lack both presentation and artistic expression. Imagine the Olympic downhill racer hurling toward the finish line at speeds exceeding 80 miles per hour. What outcome can you predict if the racer succumbs to the pressure or the pleasure? What is the penalty for wasting a precious fraction of a second on a distracting thought, fear or premature celebration? You are right, a crushing calamity is inevitable.

During the 2002 Winter Olympics, the men's downhill Gold Medal winner, Fritz Strobl, was asked if during his event, he was thinking about the "Gold." His response is enlightening. "No," he replied, "I was focusing on my skiing." Focus on the performance in front of you today and your medal will come. While in the performance mode nothing else can exist but you and the task. In order to excel, you must take charge of your ego-system. A balanced ego-system equals a powerful performance.

Remember, you are a spiritual being having a *Bodymind* experience. Keep your senses open and disciplined. Be MINDFUL but not MINDLESS. Mindful is certain and aware of reality, whereas mindless is dominated by self-criticism, doubt, and distorted perceptions. Allow the playful intent of your intuition, spontaneity, and creativity to merge and add spark to enhance the power of your performance. Here is a helpful tool to use just as you are about to enter a performance event.

Visualize the P.A.T.H.

P (passion) A (awareness) T (trust) H (honor)

Seeing is using your entire visual system to project the outcome before it happens. Visualization is a combination of imagination and memory. Imagine, for instance, solving your company's production challenge, developing new software, shooting par golf, and finding the perfect mate. Mentally picturing the result or situation that you want provides a bridge between the myriad of possibilities to the tangible manifestations. When we visualize we recall previous experiences or form entirely new ones. See it, then believe it.

The memories you have stored of moments in your life where you have already achieved success can greatly assist your present endeavor. How did you feel at the time? What was your frame of mind? What obstacles did you meet? How did you overcome them? What applies to this present performance? What did you choose to learn? What behavior did you adopt? Simply get into the same headspace and recreate the field.

(P) PASSION

Love who you are. Love what you do. You need to feel a visceral connection to the Peak Performance. When I say passion, I mean real passion, a craving, not a touchy feely fondness. It is no secret that when you love what you do, your life is transformed. You attract good things and great people into your world. All of the essential relationships in your life are re-charged. You actually enjoy your own company, you connect with people, and the world suddenly provides your heart's desire.

Also, the "fun factor" must be present. One of my friends rates all of his activities, 1 to 10, on a dimple producing scale. 1-would be having your gums scraped, 5-mildly amusing, 8 to 10-stop, I can't smile any more, or my stomach hurts from laughing so hard.

Whatever you do, do it with style and get your whole *Bodymind* and spirit around it. A playful attitude toward your business role does not mean fool heartedness or frolicking about during a board meeting with a tutu on. Serious fun is centering into the moment, fully conscious, and watching it happen.

You must love what you are doing. If you are currently in a job that you hate, don't waste your time talking or whining about it. First, find something to appreciate in your present circumstance. You must free yourself in the moment, otherwise, you will carry this pain and angst into the next job. Try changing something each day to keep it fresh. Look for some redeeming purpose. Passion empowers you to see through the hassles, disappointments, or hurts. Secondly, prepare for a change of careers. Use the "Values Assessment" portion of this workbook to help direct your vision.

During a coaching session, one of my clients disclosed that his present career path seemed blocked and that it no longer "blew his skirt up," metaphorically of course. He gave the usual reasons for staying in an unhappy situation including his time invested, benefits, age, etc. My response was, *"Life is too long to be miserable."* I then asked him to describe, in detail, his hands down, worse job ever. He told me that as a student, he took a job in a slaughterhouse one summer. The animals were hooked on an overhead conveyor assembly. His assigned task was to cut off the hoofs of each carcass as it passed overhead! Well, need I say more? It was a little much for this vegetarian to assimilate. This vivid on-going scene put his present situation in perspective. He was able to separate real suffering from his present circumstance. This gave him the room to reach for what he wanted vs. letting go of what he had.

What other things are you interested in doing? The commitment to a Peak Performance permeates all areas of your life. If you enjoy a sport or hobby, do what it takes to be proficient. You can piggyback this excellence into another area of pursuit and ignite it with a torch that is already burning. When you excel in one area, it builds global momentum. Passion is so crucial that it needs to be woven throughout the entire peak performance process. What would it take to be the very best in your profession?

(A) AWARENESS

Stay alert to everything in your inner and outer environment. Listen to all of your senses and respond to the feedback they give you. What do you see? What do you hear? What do you smell? Do you feel off balance? Are you relaxed? What is your energy level? Do you feel mentally alert? Take in everything your environment has to offer you. Your training will give you the perfect response for every situation. Some approaches would have you disassociate from your body. I prefer to gain from the experience and later understand what it meant, so that I can adequately prepare for the next performance. Log on now and download later.

(T) TRUST

This is when you really have to rely on your preparation, realizing that it can always improve. It is what it is right now, so do not choke. Feel the fear and butterflies and reach for what you want. The more you prepare and perform, the greater your certainty. Faith is fed with knowledge and results.

Believing in you comes with more effort. Learn to rely on your strengths and the soft spots take care of themselves. You are perfect by design. Read as often as needed, the Thrival Principles. Have faith that there is a natural design and destiny for your success.

(H) HONOR

What is your code of honor? What values do you live by? During every performance, you are you. What's inside comes out. Write down your code of conduct. How will you behave? Decide to be sincere, trustworthy, and honest. No matter the situation, demonstrate your courage, regardless of the outcome. Do this and you will have conquered the living death of venality. You live by a code, you suffer under capriciousness.

THE PEAK PERFORMANCE PROCESS
PHASE THREE: POLISH

The polishing phase is the time to refine your performance. This is where we separate, again, the amateurs from the professionals. Cultivating the natural perfection that lies within you is a lifetime commitment. The game of life provides plenty of abrasive challenges that generate the exact amount of heat required to cause you to shine with brilliance. Buff it up! You are the best you possible—now, let your actions show your poise and elegance.

As soon as possible, following the performance event, set aside time to reflect, renew, and respond.

This is the moment of exhilaration, the "high five" moment, the time for applause and celebration for a job well done. Take the time to enjoy the moment. This post performance afterglow is meant to be enjoyed and captured for all eternity. It is a part of your perfect design. Savor the feeling, imprint the experience deep into your psyche. Hold a "virtual" press conference and interview yourself. It might go something like this, "Well, most people thought you were going to choke. How did you pull it off? What were you thinking during the game? To what do you attribute your success? How does the world look to you from this perspective? Do you feel more courageous? Are you more optimistic?"

Remember how this moment feels for you, journal your thoughts and read them often. Conscious impressions build new neural pathways that train your nervous system for a peak readiness. Your brain begins to set aside a whole neural network designed for more frequent, brilliant performances. You are re-wiring your brain with a much clearer fiber optic system that more readily transmits the mental impulses you generate. The result is less interference and distortion between your thoughts and the amplifier of success. Remembering leads to encore performances.

The Lackluster Performance

You must embrace the reality of a lackluster or poor showing. It is possible, even with due diligent preparation. Do not torture yourself with unnecessary self-criticism. Simply reflect and contemplate the changes you wish to make. Maturity is the reliance and acceptance of your own actions.

Was the result what you had hoped for? What will you need to change? What do you wish to do over?

Mistakes occur more often than not. Relax, it is a natural and logical part of the journey. Strive for excellence in your actions. You are already perfect by nature. Say the word without attaching some big head trip to it. M-I-S-T-A-K-E. Let's not cover over this word with fluffy metaphors or new definitions. Use your mind to grasp the logical meaning of this concept by separating you, from your actions.

Whenever I want to really grasp the meaning of a word, I use the dictionary and a thesaurus. Here is what I discovered after a recent mistake. According to "Webster's College Dictionary" a mistake is an inadvertent deviation from accuracy, correctness, truth, or right conduct. An incorrect understanding, perception, or interpretation. "Roget's College Thesaurus" distinguishes a mistake from a blunder. A blunder suggests a careless, clumsy, or stupid mistake, often serious. A slip on the other hand is a small mistake. So decide which of these fit and move on.

Remember, mistakes are often your perceptions, and perceptions can be true or false. In reality, they are lessons and a learning opportunity. Learn it this time, and you will not have to repeat it. Continue to do what works, and stop doing what does not. When you accept that you will make errors, you will usually make fewer. You have been conditioned to measure yourself according to how you perform. It will take a little practice to measure yourself by who you are. The reality is that you will experience disappointments and frustrations. You are exposed to events that cause you to stumble and fall. It is part of the journey. Here is a quick post performance impression guide. Use it following your performance event or if there is a break in the action. Run through these three "A's" for perspective. What impressions are you receiving from *Bodymind* and spirit?

Acknowledge

- Acknowledge that you have the courage and discipline to risk playing the game.

- Acknowledge what you accomplished.

- Acknowledge that you have what it takes to be a polished performer.

- Acknowledge your intuition. Remember intuition is never derogatory, critical or cynical. Intuition is your inner coach and cheering section.

- Acknowledge that poor decisions, indecision, inappropriate actions, or inactions, affect your present.

Accept

- Be honest with yourself. If something was off, just say so. Denying reality creates an illusion. An illusion is seeing things that don't exist and missing things that are there. Illusions cloud the lessons and learning process.

- Accept that you may have attracted problems by persisting in your fears. What you pay attention to, manifests.

- Open to a greater level of awareness.

- Accept the responsibility, but not the blame. Perhaps you have missed a step, lost timing or have a fuzzy perspective.

- Look to see if there is something that you are not dealing with on the inside and look outside to see what you may be missing.

- Were you fully prepared?

Aspire

- After thoughtful consideration, decide the next direction to take. Will you need a new procedure, curriculum, or behavior?

- To decide literally means to "cut off from." That is to say, all other paths are closed for the moment.

- Confusion can not creep into the process.

- What do you have in your mind to do?

- Are you still determined?

- Keep focused on the goal.

- Stretch and grow through the adversity.

- See the obstacle and see through to the other side.

Examples of Applying The Peak Performance Process

I will use the game of golf and a sales presentation as examples of how to apply the Peak Performance Process.

Example #1 - Your Golf Game

Phase One: Preparation for golf

Physical

1. Ongoing
Practice on the putting green, chipping green, and driving range. Find a coach and comply with his or her lesson recommendations. Daily strength and flexibility exercises.

2. Performance Eve.
Stretch. Check equipment. Organize clothing. Set your alarm so that you can be at the course one-hour before tee time.

3. Performance Event.

Eat a high stamina meal (complex carbohydrates). Stretch. Relax on the putting green. Relax your mind. Try to "feel" your strokes. Don't "think" your way through them. Get ready to trust your learned and innate abilities.

Mental

1. Ongoing.

Read golf stories, magazine articles, lessons. Watch videos about golf. Study history. View various course layouts.

2. Performance Eve.

Review any article or video segment that inspires you. Plan for weather. Set alarm early enough so that you aren't feeling rushed.

3. Performance Event.

Visualize the course if you are familiar with it. No study or lessons today. Get into the "feeling" of the game, not the "thinking."

Spiritual

1. Ongoing.

Follow your P.A.T.H. Look for those extrasensory impressions.

2. Performance Eve.

Meditate. Pray. Find a way to center yourself. Be ready and open for intuition.

3. Performance Event.

Clear your mind for play. Expect gut feelings to guide you. Accept the guidance from the unseen caddy.

Phase Two: The Golf Performance

SEE the P.A.T.H.

SEE: Visualize the perfect tee shot. Watch the field open up. Highlight the fairway and target in your mind. Breath slowly in and out, rhythmically.

(P) Passion

Love who you are. Love what you are doing (e.g., you are a player with the time and money to hang out on the links all day). By the way, you are looking good in your well-chosen attire. What one great shot are you going to make today? You are about to step on to a beautifully manicured, living game board. You have a variety of lightening sticks, ready to crush the ball out into space.

(A) Awareness

Open your neural pathways and take in as much stimulus as you can. Be conscious of the temperature, air density, moisture content of the grass, wind force and direction, club feel, the path of the sun, the shimmering off the water hazards, the whiteness of the sand traps, the fragrance of the grass, etc. You and the course are one, not enemies.

(T) Trust

You have the training to be there. Take the time you want in between shots, there are always people pushing, that is their issue not yours. Trust the design of the ball, it's meant to fly and carry you to the green. Trust the club, it is engineered with incredible precision to make the game even easier. Trust your mind to place the ball in exactly the lie you visualize. Trust that you have the swing in you.

(H) Honor

Be trustworthy on the course. Play by the rules, even when nobody else is looking. The reality is that you will know and it will bug you and tear down all the self-view that you have been building up. Play it as it lies or take the appropriate drop. Honor your foursome, cheer for them, and wish for their best rounds.

Phase Three: Polish your golf game.

Acknowledge

- Acknowledge that one great shot. Believe in you and your game.

Accept

- Accept the responsibility for the complete collapse of your game on that hole that you double boogied.

- Decide to review your club choices and your approach strategies.

- Stretch yourself just enough past the comfort zone next time. Take the risky shots now and then.

- What is your intuition telling you about you and about your game?

- What new strategies will you prepare? Should you try a different shaft stiffness or head material?

Aspire

- Have you ever thought aloud, "If I could just get my short game together at the same time as my drives I could play professionally?" Well, you could be right.

- Commit to becoming a master.

- How good do you want to be?

Example #2: Your sales presentation

Phase One: Preparation for the Sales Performance.

Physical

1. Ongoing.
Aerobic and anaerobic exercise. Fuel for thought and concentration. Rest and breaks.

2. Performance Eve.
Flexibility/stretching exercises. Eight hours of sleep. Eat an easily digestible meal. No or minimal alcoholic beverages.

3. Performance Event.

Light workout with stretching (blood to head). Eat a power breakfast (not bacon and eggs or high sugar pancakes dripping with syrup and butter). Have something like oatmeal with honey or pure maple syrup and fresh juice.

Mental

1. Ongoing.

Study your product. Look at current research. Read books on communication styles. Read appropriate trade journals. Read books on human behavior.

2. Performance Eve.

Review your notes on the prospect. Anticipate objections. Have your briefcase and samples organized and at the door.

3. Performance Event.

Look over the presentation very briefly. Make a few notes on an index card or in your palm pilot that will inspire you. Don't listen to the news or talk radio on the way to the office. Choose music that ignites you.

Spiritual

1. Ongoing.

Attend church, pray or meditate. Look for those extrasensory impressions.

2. Performance Eve.

Meditate. Pray. Find a way to center yourself. Be ready for intuition.

3. Performance Event.

Clear your mind for play, expect gut feelings to guide you. Accept the guidance from your "sales extra-sense."

Phase Two: The Sales/Business Performance

SEE the PATH

SEE: Visualize how the presentation will unfold. See the result you would like to have happen. What are the buying signals? It can turn out exactly as you want, no objections, great commission, and a congratulatory pat on the shoulder.

(P) Passion

What do you love about you? What do you love about what you are doing at this moment? Look in the mirror. The image staring back at you is success, waiting for the chance to manifest. If not today, then definitely tomorrow. What do you love about your product or service?

(A) Awareness

Listen to your voice and your prospect's. Listen for the silence and the things not being said. Take it in and respond. If you are losing their attention, stop and ask, " I sense you're not with me. What question can I answer or what would you like to see happen?" Be flexible and alert. This person is a human being, not an enemy to conquer.

(T) Trust

You have prepared, you are the right person, and this is the correct solution for your client. There is a bonus waiting for you because of your integrity.

(H) Honor

Tell the truth. If you can say "yes" and your mind is congruent with this response then you are truthful. If, however, you say "yes" and your mind is saying"no", then you are lying. People can always find a way to deal with the truth. They are never comfortable with a lie. Under promise and over deliver.

Phase Three: Polish Your Sales Performance

Acknowledge

• Acknowledge the poise and composure that you exhibited.

• What conclusions have you come to after this performance?

• What decisions need to be made immediately?

• What do you want to follow up on?

• What feedback are you receiving from your instincts?

• Did you follow them?

- What was the result?

- Is fear shrouding the delivery?

Accept

- Were you surprised by anything in the dialogue?

- Did you feel rushed or pushed beyond your comfort zone?

- Were you too comfortable?

- Did you listen to your client or were you a babbling brook?

Aspire

- Is there some technical aspect or detail that you need to know more thoroughly?

- Strengthen the strongest part of your presentation and change the weakest link.

- What is your next goal?

- How committed are you to making the next performance event the best yet?

Allow me to share a recent Peak Performance event of my own. Two months prior to my birthday I decided it was time to run my fourth full marathon. I committed the time to train because it was of value to me. I began to apply the physical, mental and spiritual preparations we just discussed. I did not intend to fail.

On the day of the race, the weather went from wet and soggy to wind whipped pellets of rain with gusts up to 40 miles per hour. I took my place in the pack, in the dark, in the rain and began to run. It was exhilarating facing the elements with a tuned *Bodymind* and of course high-tech gear and energy bars. The first few miles of the performance were a little tougher than I had anticipated. Then I made a critical error. I started to think with each step, watching my heart monitor, listening to the timekeepers shouting out our pace. I jumped out of the moment and began to calculate how far off my intended pace I was getting. Remember, we think during the Preparation phase and the Polish phase, but never while we are IN the Performance.

My thoughts were labored and rifled with the perceptions of other racers and my own self-talk. Each mile brought me further off course and I failed to calculate a revised finish time. The support of my wife and great friends helped, but the race was still mine, time and distance. Yes, I finished the full 26.5 miles, shaken and stirred, and 35 minutes off my projected time. It was a relative failure in my mind.

The next phase is Polish. I acknowledged that I finished the race in such diverse conditions and within a reasonable time in my age group. I was grateful of the support and encouragement I had received.

Then I accepted that my thinking was infiltrated by my "rat brain" and challenged self-view.

The third consideration was to aspire to a better performance next time. I looked over my training and preparation and made important adjustments. I learned that the shock and dismay of my earlier pace times could distract my focus. Now, I am working on how to best let go of this slight control issue.

This is one example of how I use this program. Whether the performance is writing, coaching or speaking to a group, it applies in all scenarios.

PART IV
THE CIRCLE IS COMPLETE

"My momma always said that life is like a box of
chocolates, you never know what you're gonna get."

-Tom Hanks as Forrest Gump

As you engage in the process of changing YOU and YOUR
LIFE, there are a few more things you should be aware of.
There are three possible philosophies you can adopt. Before I
describe them, I would like to dispel one more piece of "myth-
information" and explain one last Thrival Principle. Many
people hold on to the ILLUSION that life is a linear
progression of successes resulting from some effort and a lot of
luck. I suspect this myth is a hallucination projected from a
collective virtual reality, and not the authentic experience of
this universe. Remember, life is punctuated by moments of
attainment and tangible rewards that happen as a result of
focused, principled effort. This unfolding play, of which you
are a part, has obstacles, disappointments, and some pain. I
know that you are already aware of this fact of life, I mention
it only as a reminder. While the universe and you are perfect,
other factors conspire at times and knock us off course. We
have discussed the need for stress and stressors to bring about
your growth changes. Since stumbling, falling, and failing are
universal experiences, I doubt that they are really accidents. It
is a part of the design. If you choose to embrace the reality of
checks and balances while in the grip of adversity, you and
your dream will prevail.

"The greatest and most important problems of life are unsolvable. They can never be solved but only out grown."

-Carl Jung

Thrival Principle #5

The final Thrival Principle is, "All processes require TIME." The Peak Performance is a Process, therefore, it is going to take time to OBTAIN and ATTAIN the life and lifestyle you are striving to create. You will need to accept that some areas in your life will move forward in quantum leaps while others are painstakingly slow. Time is relative in that there are no two journey's exactly the same. Take the TIME you need and do not measure your success by what other people are doing. Most of the time, when your efforts seem to be blocked, it is your perception of reality that has clouded an appreciation of the larger view. As your world turns and spins you off to your destination, you have three options, three separate and distinct philosophies to choose from.

1. Crisis intervention.
You can fight a continuous battle, solving one problem after another.

2. Prevent a loss.
You can look for the safe, comfortable path of least resistance.

3. Promote a gain.
You can choose to stretch and grow every fiber of your *Bodymind* and spirit, and reach for your dream.

Because your "life is too long to be miserable", this book is intended to promote your gain.

Everyone experiences setbacks and disappointments. Some of these obstacles are in your life because you are risking more. You do not construct all of the obstacles that you encounter. Stuff does happen that is not your fault, and it is your response and perceptions that will clear your way.

"All the men who signed the Declaration of Independence died in bed."

-W.R. Brock

All important endeavors have a risk. I know you have the COURAGE to live your life, not survive it. This workbook is your personal guide around and through any impediment that is thrown at you. There will be times when you doubt the wisdom of the Peak Performance Process, and even yourself. This is normal and it will pass if you stay active. When you view the successful life as a process, you will not be distracted by obstacles or concerned with trivial occurrences. Success and failure are both a part of life. It is normal to experience burnout at some point in your journey. In fact, most of my clients seek my help in some state of burnout. Burnout is a feeling of struggle, no fun, scant results. If we can use the pamper pole analogy, it is a greased OBTAIN pole that is usually the stressor. Every step up is met with a slip backwards, or, worse, you fall off the pole. If you find yourself "slip sliding away," reach for one of these principles: morality, integrity, loyalty and trustworthiness. This automatically bridges to the higher climb, that of ATTAINMENT.

When adversity is met with a renewed passionate commitment, failure is no longer an option. You must reconnect with the assessments and Peak Performance Process or you will be buried alive. There is a only a slight difference between a rut and a GRAVE. A rut is just a shallow grave. Don't fall into the rut of survival and the illusion of safety. Stay alert to the warning signs signaling trouble ahead. You now know the location of many of your life's road hazards. I also want you to know that it is impossible to remain in a state of stasis. Even when you OBTAIN the things of comfort and ATTAIN the state of consciousness wherein you are living the spiritual qualities of love and truth, it is natural and inevitable to, once again, become unbalanced and challenged. This is the perfection of the design of which you are a co-creating force.

The promise of the Peak Performance Process is that you will accomplish far more in your life if you stay on track. And, if you become lost for a time, use your personal guidance system to bring you back on course.

"Give a man a fish; you have fed him for today. Teach
a man to fish and you have fed him for a lifetime."
-Author unknown

Our relationship has matured and you now have a greater responsibility to fish for your own answers. You are well equipped and the harvest is bountiful. You will face adversity and hunger for the nourishment found only in the truth. If you become confused, disoriented, or feel weakened by any situation, seek answers to the six universal questions listed below and you will be restored. Your answers can be found in the Thrival Principles or in the other chapters. Trust your intuition. As you discover the answers on your own, it will become a part of you and nurture you all of your days.

The Six Universal Questions:

　　　1. What has happened?

　　　2. Why has it happened?

　　　3. Why to me?

　　　4. Why now?

　　　5. What will happen if I do nothing?

　　　6. What should I do about it?

Your life purpose is to restore your perfection, explore your gifts, and leave a legacy. You are the masterpiece. It is your destiny to reach for the stars and OBTAIN an abundant lifestyle. It is within you to ATTAIN a life of freedom, peace, harmony and love.

Listen to the wisdom and continue to fan the fire in your belly. You might have taken a week, a month, or even longer to read this book. It doesn't really matter. It is only important that you have continued to be connected and tuned-in. Well done. I am very proud of you and the effort you have made! Can you commit even more?

Now that you have completed the entire book, fill in the answers, once again, to the client questionnaire that you took when you began reading this book.

Client questionnaire

I want to help you achieve your next level; more fun, more profit, and more life. Please answer the following questions. Be honest. No one else will see them but you.

1. Why are you reading this book?

2. What motivates you?

3. What is your life long dream?

4. Where do you really excel?

5. Are you aware of any "soft spots" that hold you back?

6. What are some of your healthy sources of energy (exercise, proper diet, a challenge, family, spirituality, etc.)?

7. Where do you get energy that doesn't serve you, or is actually unhealthy (caffeine, competition, stress, deadlines, crisis, drugs, etc.)?

8. What consumes your time that does not give you a wonderful PRESENT or FUTURE?

9. How willing are you to make substantial changes?

10. How will you know how effective our coaching has been?

Finish the following statements:

11. If you really knew me_____

12. I am trying to give the impression that_____

13. I'm afraid you'll think I'm_____

14. I am avoiding_____

15. I want to tell you_____

Okay, we're almost done. How do your answers compare to the ones you gave when you began reading this book? Hopefully, they are different and you can use the knowledge to continue your journey and to perform at peak levels in all that you do. I would also hope that you've discovered your passion and are well on your way to fulfilling it.

Now that you've finished these questions, take just a moment longer and DESCRIBE YOUR PERFECT DAY, just as you did in the beginning of this book. Is it different? How so?

Finally, I would ask that even though you have finished reading **LIFE, The Manual,** don't just put it on the shelf with all your other books. Keep it handy. Refer to it often. Share these ideas and your own with others.

It is an honor to be your coach. I can only imagine how incredible it will be for you when *the person you are today, meets the person you are destined to be!*